For Harr,
With warm recollections and
much affection,

Victor Gollancz

FOOTPRINTS SERIES

*Jane Errington*
Editor

The life stories of individual women and men who were participants in interesting events help nuance larger historical narratives, at times reinforcing those narratives, at other times contradicting them. The Footprints series introduces extraordinary Canadians, past and present, who have led fascinating and important lives at home and throughout the world.

The series includes primarily original manuscripts but may consider the English-language translation of works that have already appeared in another language. The editor of the series welcomes inquiries from authors. If you are in the process of completing a manuscript that you think might fit into the series, please contact her, care of McGill-Queen's University Press, 1010 Sherbrooke Street West, Suite 1720, Montreal, QC H3A 2R7.

# Building Bridges

VICTOR C. GOLDBLOOM

Foreword by Graham Fraser

McGill-Queen's University Press
Montreal & Kingston · London · Ithaca

© McGill-Queen's University Press 2015

ISBN 978-0-7735-4546-5 (cloth)
ISBN 978-0-7735-8308-5 (ePDF)
ISBN 978-0-7735-8310-8 (ePUB)

Legal deposit second quarter 2015
Bibliothèque nationale du Québec

Printed in Canada on acid-free paper that is 100% ancient forest free
(100% post-consumer recycled), processed chlorine free

McGill-Queen's University Press acknowledges the support of the Canada
Council for the Arts for our publishing program. We also acknowledge
the financial support of the Government of Canada through the Canada Book
Fund for our publishing activities.

**Library and Archives Canada Cataloguing in Publication**

Goldbloom, Victor C., 1923–, author
    Building bridges / Victor C. Goldbloom.

(Footprints series; 20)
Issued in print and electronic formats.
ISBN 978-0-7735-4546-5 (bound). – ISBN 978-0-7735-8308-5 (ePDF). –
ISBN 978-0-7735-8310-8 (ePUB)

1. Goldbloom, Victor C., 1923–. 2. Jews – Québec (Province) –
Biography. 3. Pediatricians – Québec (Province) – Biography.
4. Québec (Province). Assemblée nationale – Officials and
employees – Biography. 5. Canada. Office of the Commissioner
of Official Languages – Officials and employees – Biography.
6. Québec (Province) – Biography. I. Title. II. Series: Footprints
series; 20

FC2925.1.G65A3 2015          971.4'04092          C2015-901471-9
                                                  C2015-901472-7

This book was typeset by Interscript in 11.5/14.5 Baskerville.

*To*

*Victoria and Byron, Sol and Sylvia*

*Lincoln*

*Alexandra*

*Matthew*

# Contents

# Foreword

GRAHAM FRASER
Commissioner of Official Languages

I first encountered Victor Goldbloom in the fall of 1976. He was the Minister of Municipal Affairs in Robert Bourassa's government, and I had just started as the *Maclean's* bureau chief in Montreal. I was at a restaurant, L'Aquarium, where journalists and politicians often gathered, with a group of fellow reporters from the *Tribune de la Presse* in Quebec City. Dr Goldbloom passed our table, stopped to chat, and after some encouragement, burst into a chorus, if I can remember correctly, of "'O Sole Mio!" I knew him by reputation as the man who had saved the Montreal Olympics – a reputation he modestly declines to accept in this memoir – but I had no idea of his musical talent.

The chance meeting spoke to the respect and affection with which Victor Goldbloom was treated by reporters, colleagues, and adversaries alike. That respect and affection becomes all the more understandable in this memoir. No one should read this book expecting a tell-all exercise in revealing secrets or settling scores. Dr Goldbloom spent his life, as the title suggests, building bridges; he does not blow any of them up now. Rather, it is a story of the different threads of a life dedicated to healing and reconciliation, reinforced by a love of family, music, theatre, and sport.

His father was a highly respected pediatrician, and Victor followed his path, not only as a doctor but also as a lover of music and theatre. It was an interest that crossed barriers;

Paul Robeson, the charismatic and controversial African-American bass, became a family friend, often visiting when he came to Montreal. Victor grew up in a very different Jewish Montreal from that immortalized by Mordecai Richler, but he could not avoid some of the barriers that antisemitism created, even though he was able to climb over most of them, quietly proving that excellence and charm could defeat prejudice. In life as in music, his interest was in creating harmony and resolving conflict.

Dr Goldbloom tells the inside story of his first attempt to enter politics, seeking the federal Liberal nomination in Mount Royal in 1965, and how this failure was immediately followed by success when he was elected to the Quebec legislature. His reputation for mediation and conflict resolution was such that Jean Lesage asked him to remain neutral in the 1970 leadership campaign to succeed him and to preside over the voting. Dr Goldbloom's admiration for Robert Bourassa emerges in his story of the October Crisis, and some of his details are inadvertently revealing: until then, cabinet ministers drove their own cars.

Perhaps the largest section of the book is devoted to his work in the area of interfaith dialogue, another revealing indication of his lifelong dedication to ending misunderstanding between groups and resolving conflict.

As one of Victor Goldbloom's successors as Commissioner of Official Languages, I was most interested in his chapter dedicated to the eight years he spent in the job I now hold. The speech that he gave in Edmonton in 1992 stands up, almost a quarter-century later, as a distillation of the essence and purpose of Canada's language policy.

Now in his nineties, Victor Goldbloom is as passionate and as eloquent as ever about diversity, tolerance, mutual understanding, and minority language rights. I have learned to insist that, if I share a platform with him, I should speak before he does and not after. He remains such a powerful and engaging speaker that he is, quite literally, a hard act to follow.

With this memoir, you can see why.

My paternal grandparents, Belle and Samuel Goldbloom, with my
aunt Eva on my grandmother's lap, and my father, Alton, circa 1893.
All photographs are from the Goldbloom family collection unless
otherwise stated.

My maternal grandmother,
Charlotte Ballon, in 1907.

My maternal grandfather,
Samuel Ballon, in 1907.

My great-uncle William Goldbloom in front of his store, the Prince Rupert Fur & Hide Company.

My father, Alton Goldbloom,
as a young pediatrician.

My mother, Annie
Goldbloom.

My parents, Annie and Alton Goldbloom, in their apartment in
The Trafalgar, where we held family dinners every Friday night.

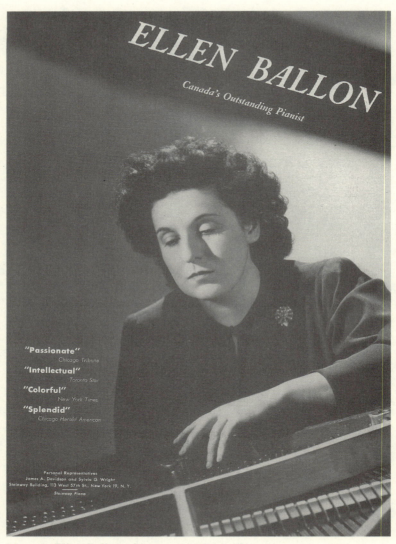

My aunt Ellen Ballon, the concert pianist, in 1944.

The home where I grew up on Crescent Street, since converted to commercial use. My father's pediatric office was on the ground floor overlooking the street. My room was on the top floor on the right.

Me as a baby in 1924.

Me on our back balcony
on Crescent Street in 1926.

Me with my father, Alton, and my brother, Richard, at Scheveningen, in the Netherlands, in 1930.

Me as a reporter at the *McGill Daily*.

Me as the Apothecary in *Romeo and Juliet*, put on by the Shakespeare Society of Montreal in 1947. Christopher Plummer played Paris and Leo Ciceri played Benvolio.

Max Slevogt's portrait of Jacob Wassermann. Charles Wassermann and I were good friends at McGill, and his father's portrait hung in our living room on Grove Park for many years.

Sheila Barshay and I were married on 15 June 1948 in New York City.

Sheila and me in front of our first apartment on Ridgewood Avenue circa 1950.

My brother, Richard, and his wife, Ruth, my parents, Annie and Alton, and Sheila and me in my parents' apartment in The Trafalgar.

My father, Alton, me, the owner of Moishes restaurant, Moishe Lighter, my mother, Annie, Sheila, the violinist Isaac Stern, my sister-in-law, Ruth, Isaac's accompanist, Shura Zakin, and my brother, Richard, at Ruby Foo's restaurant.

Three pediatricians: me, my father, Alton, and my brother, Richard.

Me with our daughter,
Susan, in 1950.

Our son Michael, our daughter, Susan, my wife, Sheila, me, and our son Jonathan.

## THE VICTOR – (DOCTOR VICTOR, THAT IS!)

Dr. Victor Goldbloom is surrounded by his admiring family after winning the Liberal nomination for the provincial riding of D'Arcy McGee on Tuesday evening. Left to right: Susan, 15; Michael, 13; Jonathan, 11, the victor, and Mrs. Goldbloom, Sheila.

Photo in the *Suburban* newspaper taken at the Duke of York's Hussars armoury in 1966, after I won the Liberal nomination in the newly formed riding of D'Arcy McGee.

Election poster, 1966.

Me with my first political mentor, Liberal leader and former premier Jean Lesage, in the National Assembly circa 1966.

# BUILDING BRIDGES

# Early Years, 1923–1939

## GROWING UP

I had the great good fortune to be born in Montreal, on 31 July 1923. My grandparents had arrived there some time before: my father's mother, Belle Goldstein, in the late 1870s as a young girl; his father, Samuel Goldbloom, in 1880 as a young man of seventeen; my mother's parents, Tsirel Klein (her children anglicized her name to Charlotte) and Samuel Ballon, in 1893 with four children in tow. They were fleeing the persecutions, discriminations, and compulsory military service of the czarist empire and the Baltic states, and they could not have known what an inspired choice they had made.

We lived downtown, on Crescent Street just below Sherbrooke. My mother's parents lived a block away, on Bishop Street. My father's parents had moved in 1912 to Vancouver, where they spent the rest of their lives.

My father, the first physician in Montreal to devote himself exclusively to pediatrics, had his office in our house. Crescent was the Harley Street of Montreal, with seventy-five doctors between Sherbrooke and St Catherine. I knew of only one French-speaking family, the Charrons. Dr Ernest Charron was the dean of Dentistry at the University of Montreal. His son André was my contemporary, and we remained friends in adult life. Later, when I became a member of the Quebec legislature and a minister, André's older sister, Louise Noël, was my good right hand and riding administrator.

There was very little contact in those days between the French-speaking and English-speaking communities. My father, however, spoke fairly good French, had a clientele that was about a third French-speaking, and decided that his two sons – my younger brother, Richard, and I – should learn French. One day in 1927 a young woman rang the doorbell, looking for a job. She was newly arrived from Paris, and someone had given her my father's name. He did not have a job to offer her, but he suggested that she come every week and converse in French with the two of us. When we started at a neighbourhood primary school, the French teacher turned out to be this young woman's sister. It was a good beginning, and I found out that I had an ear for languages and accents.

After two years, I transferred to Selwyn House School, on Redpath Street, a block and a half from our home. It was a top-notch educational experience. French was well taught, largely by a Frenchman named Michel Seymour, and I acquired a solid grounding in grammar, syntax, and vocabulary, although I was never called upon to speak the language.

The school was one – fairly common in those days – that had been founded by an individual; in this case a Mr Lucas, who had simply acquired a house and hired a number of teachers. Selwyn was very much in the British tradition, and we learned the kings and queens and the military and naval victories. There was one perfunctory year of superficial Canadian history. There were discipline, principles, and school spirit. I looked forward to every school day. The teachers made the subject matter interesting, and we could get some of them, notably Cyril Jackson and Christopher Anstey, to digress into current events. We thought we were being smart and subversive, but in fact the teachers were broadening our minds.

Selwyn House had only nine grades in those days, so I had two good years at Lower Canada College before going to McGill University. It was 1939, and World War II had just begun. The war effort required many skills, and there was pressure on the universities to graduate certain professionals, including physicians, more quickly. I was admitted to medicine after only three years of science, and the four-year medical program was compressed into three, so I was barely twenty-two when I got my degree.

The Montreal Children's Hospital (it was called the Children's Memorial Hospital in those years, having been founded in 1904 as a memorial to Queen Victoria, who had died three years earlier) accepted me as a junior intern. After two years, I went to the Babies' Hospital in New York for a further year and a half.

My father had a very good friend, Dr Murray Bass, who was head of Pediatrics at New York's Mount Sinai Hospital, and it was in the home of Dr and Mrs Bass that I met Sheila Barshay, to whom I proposed only three months later. I was impressed by her education – she had graduated that spring from Mount Holyoke College, the oldest women's university in North America – and by her work with the League of Women Voters of New York State. She had a notable social conscience, which attracted me enormously, and she opened thought processes that had been latent until then. We went to the theatre, to the opera (*Der Rosenkavalier* at the Met), to museums, to concerts, and to baseball games. We were married at the Society for the Advancement of Judaism, the founding synagogue of the Reconstructionist Movement and a place of outstanding intellectual stimulation, and in January 1949 we settled in Montreal.

## FAMILY ANTECEDENTS

My mother, Annie Esther Ballon, was the fourth of seven children. Two of her brothers, David and Harry, became doctors and one, Isidore, a lawyer; her sister Ellen was a concert pianist. There were two other sisters, Miriam (called Mamie) and Florence. My father was the eldest of three – except that he was not. Three earlier siblings, including twins, had died at very young ages. Superstition dictated that he be named Abraham Isaac after the patriarchs, but that those names never be used except in the synagogue, so that evil spirits would be unable to find him. He was instead called Alter, the old one – in the hope that he would live to a ripe old age – and this was anglicized to Alton, probably in honour of an (unsuccessful but much respected) American presidential candidate, Judge Alton B. Parker.

My father was inspired to study medicine by an exceptional role model, Dr William Molson. Dr Molson, whose house at Sherbrooke Street and McGill College Avenue has been preserved as a historic site, was a much beloved physician who gave great consideration to families of limited economic means and had many patients in the Jewish community. At a very young age, my father came down with a severe pneumonia, causing devastating anxiety to his parents, who had already lost three children. Antibiotics were a half-century in the future, and Dr Molson spent long hours at my father's bedside providing the limited therapeutic measures that were available at the time. My father never forgot him and forever cherished his memory and his example.

I was unusual among my contemporaries because my father had been born in Montreal. My mother liked to say that she had been also, but in fact she had arrived from Lithuania in 1893 at the age of two. My maternal grandparents were religiously observant; my paternal ones were not, but were fully identified with the Jewish community. My mother kept a kosher home, in good measure out of respect for her parents; my father was, as he was inclined to say, gastronomically relaxed. We observed the holidays, Miss Luba Gordon came in weekly to give us Hebrew lessons – I became fairly fluent – and I went to synagogue rather regularly, usually walking there and back with my grandmother. After my bar mitzvah, I became a cantor in the Junior Congregation.

My brother, Richard, not quite a year and a half younger, was a freer spirit than I and had a ready sense of humour. He went to the same schools, also became a pediatrician, and in 1967 moved to Halifax to become head of the newly constructed Izaak Walton Killam Hospital for Children. He contributed significantly to the development of pediatric care in Nova Scotia and later served as chancellor of Dalhousie University. He married Ruth Miriam Schwartz of New Waterford, Nova Scotia, a McGill graduate in physical education who later became celebrated as the creator of the national immigration museum, Halifax's Pier 21. They were both deservedly made members of the Order of Canada.

My paternal grandparents would visit from time to time, and although the contacts were infrequent, our relationship was especially warm. We travelled occasionally to Vancouver, and I have some recollection of five nights and four days on the train in 1929. We also were passengers on an early flight of Trans-Canada Airlines, which later became Air Canada. The ten-seat plane stopped in Ottawa, Toronto, North Bay, Kapuskasing, Winnipeg, Regina, and Lethbridge (where the Rockies are lower than at Calgary and Edmonton). I remember my grandparents' house on Nanton Avenue, in Shaughnessy Heights, and my Uncle Tevye's and Aunt Anne's home on West King Edward, with loganberry bushes lining the back lawn. My Aunt Eva (my father's sister) and Uncle Moe Brotman also lived in Vancouver, but later moved to San Francisco. We always looked forward to these encounters.

My grandmother Belle Goldbloom was an exceptional knitter, and until she was very old, I never had a store-bought sweater. My grandfather was a travelling salesman, carrying watches and jewellery all over Western Canada. He eventually was awarded a pass on the Grand Trunk Railway. His greatest pleasure was to be in a given city at the same time as my father, whom he would introduce with inordinate pride to the other travelling salesmen in the hotel lobby.

My grandfather Goldbloom had an older brother named William. He had earlier lived in Montreal, Winnipeg, and Vancouver, but he was a frontiersman who always moved on as civilization approached. When I met him, he had settled in Prince Rupert, in northern British Columbia, leaving his wife and two daughters behind. He traded in furs and had a store in front of which was a sawed-off tree trunk embraced by a stuffed bear. His stationery had a picture of it, with the caption "Bear in mind Goldbloom ..." His language was uninhibitedly salty, as was his behaviour. My mother would cringe every time he showed up at our door, which he sometimes did unannounced. He looked for all the world like Colonel Harland Sanders of Kentucky Fried Chicken fame, and I wish I had known him better.

My Ballon grandparents, living just a block away in Montreal, were part of my daily life. My grandfather was a recycling pioneer – he collected scrap metal for re-smelting – and somehow made enough to buy a three-storey house and put his three sons through professional education. Learning was valued above everything else and was worth every possible sacrifice. A later business venture was a broom factory. Wiped out by the 1929 crash, my grandfather decided to retire, and he and my grandmother were dependent on their children for the rest of their lives.

## THE SOCIETY IN WHICH I LIVED

The society in which I grew up was, to use a gentle word, compartmentalized. Religion was a determinant of social status and of career opportunities. The Anglo-Saxon Protestant domination of the economy and the financial world provided no openings for those of other origins. Provincial politics, on the other hand, although not impervious to high-level anglophone influence, was overwhelmingly francophone. Social services and cultural organizations were Catholic, Protestant, or Jewish. Widespread uniligualism was severely limiting to French-English communication.

Antisemitism was something that everyone took for granted. To be Jewish was to live with restrictions and prejudices, to face doors that were shut and obstacles that were discriminatory. To be Christian was to consider anti-Jewish phraseology a part of normal discourse. A few individuals, my parents among them, gained a certain degree of partial acceptance. I benefited from it. (Prejudice tended to be set aside when a good doctor was being sought.) McGill University admitted Christians with 600 marks out of 1,000 in its matriculation examinations. Jews had to get 750 and were subject to quotas in faculties such as Medicine. (So were women.) There were hotels and resorts where one could not go, organizations one could not join, and promotions one could not obtain. I resented these obstacles, but I learned to find ways of contributing to society in spite of them.

Life was nevertheless agreeable, and overt antisemitism was fairly uncommon. As time went by, my parents achieved an appreciable degree of recognition. My father acquired an international reputation, was one of a bare half-dozen Jewish members of the medical faculty at McGill, and was beloved by his patients of both languages and all three religions.

My mother, brought up in rather modest circumstances, taught herself to be an expert in etiquette. As a thirty-year-old, she had been chosen to head the women's auxiliary of the Montreal Hebrew Maternity Hospital (where I was born), and she was therefore the natural choice to be the founding president of the Women's Auxiliary of the Jewish General Hospital when it came into being in 1934. The J G H Auxiliary became the most dynamic in the city, and a relationship developed with those of other hospitals. My mother came to play a leading role, convening meetings in our home and devising ways in which auxiliaries could help their hospitals. Her religion seemed not to be an issue.

That had special significance, because prejudice had been the reason for the creation of the Jewish General Hospital. My father, my uncle Dr David Ballon, their friend Dr Harold Segall, and a very few others had achieved staff positions in McGill's teaching hospitals, but many competent physicians had not. No school of nursing – not one – would accept a young Jewish woman as a student. The JGH made a professional career possible.

My father's stature was not, however, sufficient for McGill in 1938. Through the first third of the twentieth century, Pediatrics had been a sub-department of Medicine. A sustained effort had been mounted, under the leadership of Dr Harold Cushing, an old-fashioned gentleman and an extraordinary fountain of clinical knowledge, to give Pediatrics autonomy. That was finally achieved in 1937.

Dr Cushing was then sixty-two years old. Retirement age was rigidly fixed at sixty-three. McGill wrestled with the dilemma: should it appoint Dr Cushing, in recognition of his leadership and his prestige, for a single year? Or should it immediately name a younger man (not a woman, in those days!) who would have a longer time frame in which to build the new department of Pediatrics? They chose Dr Cushing. That meant that a year later, in 1938, the position would be vacant. In all objectivity, my father was the person of international stature, the intellectual leader of the field, and the most visionary of the potential candidates. Nonetheless, he was passed over. Dr Rolf Struthers, who was chosen, continued to hold the position even after he volunteered for military service and went overseas. A position of acting pediatrician-in-chief was created, and it was occupied for a time by my father, notwithstanding his earlier rejection!

The war ended. Dr Struthers decided to resign and to take on a position with the United Nations. This time my father was appointed. When he arrived in the pediatrician-in-chief's office, there was a small pile of accumulated correspondence. One of the letters was from the pediatrician-in-chief at the University of Toronto. A recent graduate had asked him for a letter of recommendation for an internship position at the Children's. The letter, addressed to my father's predecessor, read, "I am informed that Dr X has applied for an internship position at your hospital. I understand that he is of the Jewish faith. I think nothing more need be said. Sincerely, ..."

I personally encountered little overt antisemitism in school. I recall a single episode of derogatory language in my second or third year at Selwyn House and none at Lower Canada College. McGill proved generally welcoming. Officially a Jew could not get elected to the executive of the Students' Society, but I managed to serve there for a year or so because someone resigned, no one paid attention to the by-election call, and I got in by acclamation. When the next regular election rolled around, I was of course defeated. I thought, however, that I had made a point: that penetrating this bastion had been important and that people had discovered that I was a student like anyone else. I became a senior editor of the *McGill Daily*, produced two student variety concerts in support of the Canadian Red Cross, and chaired a major conference on Canada and the postwar world. McGill was beginning to change, and after the war the discriminatory differential for admission was abolished, and a Jew was elected president of the Students' Society.

## BASEBALL AND OTHER SPORTS

My parents had great interest in culture, but none whatsoever in sports. They were, however, supportive of my participation in sports at school. I played cricket – not very well – soccer, where I discovered that I was fast on my feet, and hockey. As well, it was a Selwyn House tradition that everyone competed in at least one event in the annual track and field day in June. I developed a bit of talent as a sprinter, and when I got to Lower Canada College, I was able both years to win the 100-, 220-, and 440-yard dashes.

At about ten years of age I was afflicted by a recurrent outbreak of staphylococcal infections (boils). There were no antibiotics in those days, and injections of a staphylococcal vaccine, variably successful, were the only known treatment. Rest was considered essential, so my hockey career was put on

hold – until I persuaded my parents that goaltending was a
sedentary occupation. I became the backup goaltender on
the school team.

I went whenever I could to the Forum to watch the Canadiens
and my favourites, the Montreal Maroons. I saw Howie Morenz,
Aurèle Joliat, Johnny "Black Cat" Gagnon, Hooley Smith,
Jimmy Ward, Baldy Northcott, Lionel Conacher, and the solid
goaltender Alec Connell, the "Ottawa Fireman." Later it was
Rocket Richard, Toe Blake, Doug Harvey, and the incomparable Jean Béliveau, whom I had the privilege of getting to know
after his hockey career was over and he devoted himself to
community endeavours. What is striking, in retrospect, is how
representative both of these teams were of Montreal. The
Canadiens were indeed the "Flying Frenchmen," with Pit
Lépine, Georges and Sylvio Mantha, and Albert "Battleship"
Leduc. But Doug Harvey, Dickie Moore, and Gerry McNeil
were also homegrown stars who were still part of the community after their playing days were over.

Tennis also became an interest, and over the years I have
followed the careers of Björn Borg, Roger Federer, Althea
Gibson, Billie Jean King, and Martina Navratilova. One summer in the 1930s a Davis Cup tie between Australia and Japan
was played at the Mount Royal Tennis Club on Grey Avenue,
and I was enthralled as Adrian Quist and John Bromwich
eked out a difficult win.

I never played football, but I followed the McGill Redmen. I
was in the stands for the 1938 championship game, which they
won 9-0. It was actually a close and tense struggle, with virtually
no first downs, so it was repeatedly two plays and a kick, and
Herby Westman, the McGill punter, gained about five yards
on each exchange until he was able to kick nine single points
into the end zone. Of course I also became attached to Sam
Etcheverry, Herb Trawick, and the Alouettes.

Baseball, however, was my passion. My uncle Harry Ballon,
my mother's youngest brother, took me to my first games in
1931. The Montreal Royals played at Delorimier Stadium,

and some years I saw almost half their home games. In 1932 the Philadelphia Athletics came to town for an exhibition game. They had won the World Series in 1929, 1930, and 1931, so it was a momentous occasion. The Royals beat them 4-2, but the Athletics gave us the special privilege of seeing Robert Moses "Lefty" Grove, to many people the best pitcher who ever played, pitch the eighth and ninth innings. He was untouchable.

The Royals had a centre fielder named Jimmy Ripple, who specialized in making easy catches look dramatic; he eventually made it to the majors. There were veterans like Woody Jensen and Curt Davis, who nailed down a Little World Series (the championship of the two top minor leagues) with a tight 2-0 victory. And there was "Sunday Gus" Dugas, who would generally manage, in the course of a Sunday doubleheader, to hit a home run over the scoreboard.

The scoreboard was in right field, rather high – somewhat like the left-field "Green Monster" in Boston's Fenway Park – but only 293 feet down the foul line. Behind it, across Parthenais Street, was the Grover Mills factory, with a sign carrying the slogan "Knit to Fit." A ball that cleared the scoreboard would land on the factory roof, so when Gus Dugas came to bat, the fans, of both languages, would chant in unison, "Knit to Fit! Knit to Fit!"

I saw Jackie Robinson make his debut in a Royals uniform, playing so brilliantly that he went up to the major league Brooklyn Dodgers the following year, but first helping the Royals win the Little World Series. Because he was the first African American to play in organized baseball (apart from the Negro leagues), there was concern about his acceptance. Montreal welcomed him with open arms, not only the fans at Delorimier Stadium but his French-Canadian neighbours on De Gaspé Street and the population in general. I was proud of our city and our team.

I followed major league baseball quite intently. I remember Carl Hubbell, one of my favourites, pitching the New York

Giants to a World Series win over the Washington Senators in 1933. A good many years later I sat in the old Polo Grounds and watched Hubbell, in the twilight of his career, craft an 8-4 victory over the Pittsburgh Pirates, helped by a Mel Ott home run. But I became a Yankee fan. Joe DiMaggio was my hero, and I admired Lou Gehrig, Bill Dickey, Tommy Henrich, Yogi Berra, Allie Reynolds, and Phil Rizzuto. I was there in the far reaches of the left-field stands for the fifth game of the 1956 World Series, Don Larsen's perfect game. I had two tickets, and I invited my friend Norman Redlich, who was later a senior lawyer for the Warren Commission (which investigated the Kennedy assassination) and then for the City of New York, and dean of the New York University Law School. Norman was a Dodger fan, and as I was biting my nails with each Larsen pitch, Norman was muttering, "What's wrong with us, we can't get a hit?"

And of course when the Montreal Expos came along, I became a faithful follower, first in the intimacy of Jarry Park and then at the Olympic Stadium. I watch less baseball now, although the World Series still magnetizes me, as it did in my adolescent days, when I would slip out of the synagogue for a couple of hours on Yom Kippur afternoon to listen to it on the radio. What is it about baseball which so captivates me? Certainly, the intellectual challenge of baseball strategy, but also the beauty of the flight of the ball, the drama of a close game, and the attractiveness of the setting. Statistics and records of achievement – and the certainty of most, but not all, of them being broken one day – are endlessly fascinating. I would rather watch it – and play it – than any other sport.

# Special Friendships

## HUGH MACLENNAN

I met Hugh MacLennan when I arrived at Lower Canada College in 1937. He was just thirty years old and had recently come on staff as a teacher. He was not a professional educator or pedagogically outstanding – others like Robert Speirs, who later became head of Selwyn House, had more of a knack – but he was far and away the most impressive intellectual presence on the faculty.

Hugh taught Latin, a subject in which I had received a very thorough grounding from Cyril Jackson at Selwyn House and was able to hold my own, and this made for stimulating discussions and excursions into literature. He also offered Greek as an extra, and I signed up for a year. Both languages were later of immense help to me in understanding medical terminology. Hugh's style was dry and pleasantly serious. I liked and admired him, and was drawn to him as a person. A number of us formed a discussion group that we named the Socratic Club, and Hugh became our mentor. He was present at all our meetings, and the topics were often his suggestions, but he was a background resource rather than a director, and he significantly broadened our horizons.

In addition to speaking the ancient classical languages, he was particularly knowledgeable about the Greek and Roman civilizations and especially about their governmental structures. He would discourse about Canadian, British, and American democracies and relate their principles, mechanisms, and balances to those of ancient Greece and Rome. Some people found this a bit dry, but I was captivated by its pertinence and benefited from it later in public life. As well, it drew me closer to Hugh. When I graduated from Lower Canada and started at McGill, I came up with the idea of spending some formal time with him, sitting at the feet of the master and absorbing wisdom and an understanding of the world. I was not sure that my parents would buy it, but they did, and I would go over to the MacLennans' apartment on Mountain Street just above Dorchester and essentially just listen.

Hugh's wife, Dorothy Duncan, who also became a respected writer, was warmly welcoming. She was a big person, in body and in spirit. Hugh disguised her as a small woman in *The Watch That Ends the Night*, the late semi-autobiographical novel that has a character modelled on the controversial doctor Norman Bethune, but he accurately portrayed her "voice like a cello" and the recurrent life-threatening illness she did her best to ignore. She did not participate in our conversations, but she clearly absorbed their content and would often send me on my way with a pertinent observation.

Gradually, the sixteen-year gap in age between Hugh and myself became insignificant and a real friendship evolved. Our circles would intersect fairly often, and as I moved into public life, Hugh had thoughtful comments to offer, always perceptive and sometimes pungent. He gave our relationship a new balance and sought my opinions and analyses. My affection deepened and deepened.

Hugh MacLennan became a distinguished writer. His seven novels, beginning with *Barometer Rising*, raised Canadian fiction to a new level. (I subsequently put Alice Munro on an equal pedestal.) His collections of essays – *Cross Country*, *Thirty and Three*, and *Scotchman's Return* – are among Canada's best nonfiction. I cherish his memory. For over seventy-five years I have boasted of being Hugh's first publisher. In 1937–38 I was chosen to be senior editor of the Lower Canada College school magazine. There was traditionally a "Masters' Section," and I canvassed teachers for contributions. Hugh came through with an account of the explosion of the munitions ship *Mont Blanc* in Halifax harbour in 1917 and the massive devastation of the city. Two years later it became the centrepiece of *Barometer Rising*, and his literary career was on its way.

MacLennan is particularly remembered for *Two Solitudes* and is even thought to have coined the phrase. The novel deals with the tensions and communication barriers between French-speaking and English-speaking Quebec, and the words are understood as denoting a barrier that few on either side were able to cross or even to see beyond. In fact, the dedication of the book – "To Dorothy Duncan with admiration and love" – is from the German poet Rainer Maria Rilke:

Love consists in this,
that two solitudes protect,
and touch, and greet each other.

### CHARLES WASSERMANN

My best friend at McGill was Charles Wassermann. He had grown up in Austria, and he was one of those young men who, when World War II broke out, was attending school in England and, because he had an Austrian passport, was deemed an enemy alien, taken into custody, and sent into internment in Canada. Through the efforts of the Jewish community, these young Austrians and Germans were, after some time, released under the sponsorship of local families and allowed to attend school or university. Charles was at Lower Canada College, in my brother's class, when I first met him; then he came to McGill, and the chemistry of friendship developed.

My German was limited, but he became *Wasserstoff* (hydrogen) and I was *Superoxid* (peroxide). We worked together on the *McGill Daily*, acted with the McGill Players' Club, and devoted a good deal of time to the McGill Radio Workshop, which Charles founded. He had friends at the Canadian Broadcasting Corporation, primarily but not only in the International Service (where he did some German-language broadcasting), and he was able to arrange for studio time for recording plays, some of which were written by our members. The C B C aired several of them, and at least one of our alumni, Don Cameron, went on to a professional radio career as a top-notch announcer. Another, Griffith Brewer, went into the theatre as an actor and a backstage professional. We wrote a McGill Radio Workshop hymn, sung to the tune of "Rock of Ages":

C B C , we pray to thee,
Let us use your Studio C.
But in charging, please be prudent,
Even Goldbloom is a student.
C B C , we pray to thee,
Let us use your studio, free!

(Names were interchangeable, but mine was the convenient one with two syllables.)

Charles's father, who died in December 1934, was the celebrated German Jewish author Jakob Wassermann. (Charles's mother was not Jewish, and he had no Jewish upbringing.) Jakob Wassermann had written and spoken polemically against Hitler, and he was a marked man when the Nazis came to power. When he died, one of the valuable things he left behind was a portrait painted of him by the noted German artist Max Slevogt.

The Wassermanns were living at that time in the small Austrian village of Alt-Aussee, not far from Salzburg. The village was at the dead end of a valley, backed against impassable mountains. Their house, beside a small lake, was the only impressive residence. Mrs Wassermann reasoned that if the Nazis came – which they did after the *Anschluss* in 1938 – they would know whose house it was and would surely destroy the portrait. Her brother, the well-known actor Oskar Karlweis (who after the war appeared on Broadway, notably as Jacobowsky in *Jacobowsky and the Colonel*), had a substantial house in Vienna that was full of art, and she felt that the portrait would be less conspicuous and less identifiable there. She and Charles moved in with him, bringing the painting with them.

One afternoon they came back from shopping and found the frame lying in the courtyard and the painting gone. They assumed that the Nazis had identified the portrait and would promptly destroy it. The situation worsened, and they left for Italy and then for Britain, where Charles was enrolled in school. His mother, who was a lay psychoanalyst trained by Carl Gustav Jung, moved to Ottawa and opened a practice there.

The war ended, and one day she received a letter from British friends who had travelled to the Continent. They told her how pleased they had been to see her husband's portrait in the archbishop's palace in Salzburg. The theft had clearly been the work of ordinary art thieves, who had been interrupted before they could take any other paintings from the Karlweis collection, and who had sold it on the black market.

She wrote to the archbishop. He replied considerately, saying that there was a ten-year statute of limitations in Austria and the portrait belonged to him, but that because of who she was, he would send it to her on the condition that it would revert to him upon her death. It arrived in Ottawa three days before she was to leave for Europe to visit her two daughters from a previous marriage. She opened the crate to verify that it was indeed the Slevogt portrait and left on her journey. Unfortunately, while in Europe, she died.

Charles was her heir. Sadly, he had developed diabetes some years before, and it had not been well controlled. It had affected his eyesight, and he was unable to see the portrait. Also, as a result of his illness, he was uninsurable. The portrait was thus

his only provision for his old age and for his wife, Jacqueline.
He died at a relatively early age, after a brilliant career, notwith-
standing his blindness, as European correspondent for the
Canadian Broadcasting Corporation.

Charles, with Jacqueline, had moved back to Alt-Aussee.
Afraid of what would happen to the painting if he brought
it to Austria, he asked us to keep it for him. It hung over our
fireplace mantel for many years. Eventually, after Charles's
death, Jacqueline found a home for it in a museum of German
literature in Marbach am Neckar, a small town just north of
Stuttgart. Some years later, after Jacqueline's death, we made
a pilgrimage to see it. It had never been our property, but we
felt it was part of our family.

# The Arts

## MUSIC

There were musical genes on both sides of my family. My father's younger brother, Tevye, was a violinist who did a stint with the Vancouver Symphony. Four of my mother's six siblings were also musical. Harry and Florence, the twins, who were the youngest, played the violin and the cello respectively. Isidore, the second oldest, a lawyer by profession, was not a performer but had deep musical knowledge; he took over as my piano teacher after many years of pedestrian lessons and opened the world of Mozart, Beethoven, and Brahms to me. The star, however, was my aunt Ellen, several years younger than my mother, who had brilliant talent and became a professional pianist.

Ellen Ballon gave her first recital at the age of six, with special pedals to reach her short legs. The mayor of Montreal lifted her onto the piano stool. As she pursued her studies, she came to the attention of leading teachers, including the great Polish pianist Josef Hofmann, with whom she spent two summers in Switzerland. When World War I broke out in 1914, she, with my twenty-three-year-old mother as her chaperone, were at the Hofmanns' in Vevey and had a tense time getting back home.

Ellen's career took off, and she did command performances for British royalty and for the Roosevelts at the White House.

She met prominent American families and was entertained, and sometimes sponsored, by them. The glamour of these relationships tended to diminish her work ethic, but she did achieve a fairly significant career. In her later years she met the Brazilian composer Heitor Villa-Lobos, and he wrote a piano concerto, which he dedicated to her; she played it with a number of orchestras in different parts of the world.

Ellen actively supported McGill University's Faculty of Music and is warmly recalled in its annals. Although she came to live primarily in New York City, she was periodically in Montreal and had a small suite in the Ritz-Carlton Hotel with her own piano. She was a *grande dame* with a larger-than-life personality, and her flamboyant presence was never unnoticed.

The professional colleague with whom she had the most special relationship was the great bass-baritone Paul Robeson. Paul toured the world extensively and would ask another artist to share his programs. Ellen was that artist for some time, and eventually she introduced him to her family. He became a genuine friend.

Paul was a giant of a man, a football hero at Rutgers. He was perhaps the most prominent African American of his time, a militant opponent of the generalized discrimination that he and his people faced, and he made himself controversial by supporting left-wing causes and, for a time, expressing admiration for the Soviet Union (where he said he found easier acceptance). He gave fairly frequent recitals in Montreal, and there was always a conspicuous police presence along the walls. Being his friend was not generally well regarded, but my parents were unhesitatingly so.

Robeson gave a concert in Montreal in 1945 and took time to come to my Ballon grandparents' home. My grandmother had died, and my grandfather's mobility had decreased so that he passed his days sitting in a chair in his bedroom. Paul went in to see him alone and spent perhaps fifteen minutes chatting. Then he said that, before he left, he would like to sing something for my grandfather, and we listened raptly to "The Kaddish of Rabbi Ben Ezra," which ends movingly with the traditional Hebrew (actually Aramaic) words "Yitgadal ve-yitkadash shemei rabbah" (May the great name of God be magnified and sanctified), the mourner's prayer.

Another very special relationship for our family was with the outstanding violinist Isaac Stern. Born in Russia, he had come to San Francisco at an early age. He was still young when his father died, and his mother matriarchally took up the development of his career. She found a friend in my father's sister Eva (one of my favourite people), and we met Mrs Stern and Isaac on one of our occasional visits to the West Coast. A lifelong friendship was launched.

Isaac's accompanist was the pianist Alexander (Shura) Zakin, somewhat older and to some extent a father figure. Shura tended to have a serious demeanour, which concealed a dry and imaginative sense of humour, and he was very much a part of our friendship. Whenever we could, we travelled to places where the two were giving a recital or Isaac was playing with an orchestra, as, for example, when he premiered a violin concerto by the American composer and teacher William Schuman with the Boston Symphony. Isaac had been a young prodigy and had curtailed his general education to concentrate on his musical career, but he was brilliantly intelligent and observant and had perceptive things to say about the cities, countries, and people he visited. After almost every concert, we would have the pleasure of spending the late evening with him and usually with Shura.

My own musical interest began when my father started bringing home phonograph records. I was drawn to the classics, helped by my uncle Isidore and occasionally by my aunt Ellen, and I became fairly knowledgeable. My choice of New York for my pediatric residency was significantly motivated by two of my passions, music and baseball – by access to Carnegie Hall and to Yankee Stadium. My piano lessons did not make me a virtuoso, but I discovered that I had a voice, a bass-baritone much deeper than my speaking register. I took up Schubert lieder and Italian (and other) opera, and was bold enough to give occasional recitals. I looked after the children of Noel Talarico, who had a semi-classical orchestra that was much in demand, and whenever he spotted me, he brought me up on the stage to sing "'O Sole Mio!" and Ruggiero Leoncavallo's "Mattinata."

My models, of a quality beyond my reach, were Alexander Kipnis, an incomparable singing actor, and Ezio Pinza, whom I once interviewed. I admired Salvatore Baccaloni's Leporello in *Don Giovanni* and later Jerome Hines's Gurnemanz in *Parsifal.* I became an opera buff and in later years relished the live televised performances from the Metropolitan in New York: the close-ups, the translated subtitles, and of course the great singing. The human voice is, for me, the most expressive musical instrument of all.

## THE THEATRE

The theatrical genes were all on my father's side of the family. As he recounts in his autobiography, *Small Patients,* he and his lifelong best friend, S.N. (Sam) Behrman, who stayed in the theatre and became a noted Broadway playwright, spent some months touring with a stock company on the Radio Keith Orpheum (R K O) circuit. My father played bit parts, sometimes without lines – in one play he was a sheriff's deputy who tacked up a "Wanted Man" poster on one side of the proscenium arch, crossed the stage, and tacked up the same poster in Yiddish (this was considered hilarious by early-twentieth-century audiences). Since he never got to be Hamlet or Othello or Romeo, he decided that pediatrics was a better career choice.

His sister Eva also did some acting. Both of them had prepared by taking what were called elocution lessons, which taught the proper pronunciation of words and the proper pitching of the voice. My father would quote one of the exercises, a poem to be enunciated slowly and clearly with a plummy British accent:

When I asked her to wed, "Go to father," she said.
Now, she knew that I knew that her father was dead;
And she knew that I knew what a life he had led;
So she knew that I knew what she *meant* when she said,
"Go to father."

For all his life, however, my father remained a student of the theatre. In 1932 he published, in a leading pediatric journal, a scholarly paper on pediatric references in the plays of Shakespeare. In those days our family took substantial summer holidays, generally across the Atlantic, and we went several times to the Shakespeare Memorial Theatre in Stratford-upon-Avon, a memorable experience. Broadway was also a frequent destination, and travelling companies would often visit Montreal.

At McGill I rose to be theatre critic of the *Daily*. I joined the McGill Players' Club and played leads in James Bridie's *What Say They?* and in *The Male Animal* by James Thurber and Elliot Nugent. At the Montreal Repertory Theatre I snagged a substantial part in S.N. Behrman's *Biography*, under Herbert Whittaker's direction, with the great Betty Wilson in the leading role, which had been created by Ina Claire on Broadway. Again under Herbert Whittaker's direction, I played a Hungarian professor of anatomy with the YM-YWHA Players in a drama called *The Burning Bush* and the son in Robert E. Sherwood's *There Shall Be No Night,* which had starred Alfred Lunt and Lynn Fontanne in New York. A Shakespeare Society of Montreal came into being, and I appeared in two of its three productions, playing the Apothecary and the leading minuet dancer in *Romeo and Juliet* and Claudio in *Much Ado About Nothing*, directed by Roberta Beattie.

During my years on the *Daily*, I was able, often with Sam Behrman's help, to get interviews with theatre luminaries, including the celebrated playwright Maxwell Anderson (who reputedly never gave interviews) and the crusty Alexander Woollcott, who came to Montreal to play Sheridan Whiteside, the character modelled on himself, in George S. Kaufman and Moss Hart's *The Man Who Came to Dinner*.

Like my father, I gave up the theatre for the practice of pediatrics, but I remained an aficionado. When the Stratford Shakespearean Festival was launched in Stratford, Ontario, Sheila and I started the tradition of an annual pilgrimage, and we included our children from the age of six on. One of my fellow actors from McGill, Leo Ciceri, became a leading Stratford player, and we would visit with him each year until his untimely death in an automobile accident. Another, Christopher Plummer, who had been, at the age of sixteen, the County Paris in *Romeo and Juliet* when I had been the Apothecary, went on to even greater stardom. When, in recent years, Sheila and I went to Stratford-upon-Avon, the Old Vic in London, and the reconstituted Globe Theatre in Southwark, we concluded that our festival in Ontario is now the best Shakespeare in the world.

It seems to me that live theatre is undervalued and under-used in our education systems. Studying a play from a book is simply not the same as seeing it on the stage. Watching a play can be wonderful, but acting can help us develop the projection of our voice, the carriage of our body, and the effectiveness of our communication. Theatre teamwork is also valuable training for life in general. Theatre helps us understand human relations, human history, and the world. Indeed, when I was Commissioner of Official Languages, I commissioned a play for school audiences which dealt, through the eyes of a couple of young people, with the history of Canada as a two-language country. It was written by Canadian playwright Anne Chislett and was taken on tour by Geordie Productions of Montreal under the inspired direction of Elsa Bolam.

The theatre is an enduring passion for many, many people, and I am gratefully convinced that my own experience has helped me to be an effective speaker and communicator and has enhanced my understanding of human nature.

## FINE ARTS

There were no artists in my family – until my granddaughter Victoria Restler came along – but art appreciation was a conspicuous value. (When Sheila and I became engaged, I got to know her maternal grandfather, Samuel Reich, a low-key and agreeable person who was a prolific painter in the "naïve" style which was made famous by Grandma Moses.)

Between 1928 and 1936, my father organized half a dozen family vacations in Europe, and in each city we devoted a good deal of time to the principal art museum or museums. We became acquainted with Rembrandt and Van Dyck and Frans Hals, with Botticelli and Raphael and Canaletto, with Gainsborough and Constable. The French Impressionists were a later discovery, and I developed a lifelong attachment to Claude Monet, whose production was enormous, and even more to Alfred Sisley, whose output was comparatively limited. I came to admire Édouard Manet and his sister-in-law Berthe Morisot, who married his brother Eugène and was the only woman among the six founders of the Impressionist movement.

In 1930 and again in 1931, we spent a week at the Grand Hotel in Scheveningen, a seaside suburb of The Hague. There was a small art shop in the lobby, run by a woman named Henriette Blommers and featuring the work of her father, Bernardus Johannes, who had been a middle-rank member of The Hague School with Jozef Israels and the Maris brothers and had died in 1914. She still had a number of his works, some of them unfinished and unsigned, and my father brought home two excellent paintings and four charcoal drawings.

My father took a certain interest in Canadian painting. The Group of Seven had held its first exhibition in 1920 – Tom Thomson, who was not a member but is often mentioned in conjunction with them, had died in 1917 – but their full celebrity was still in the future. An Eastern Townships painter named

Frederick Simpson Coburn, whose specialty was horse-drawn vehicles on snow-covered roads, was fairly well-known, and my father purchased *On the Richmond Road,* which was a bit special in that the sleigh had two horses whereas Coburn usually painted only one. We still have it.

With time, the Group of Seven reached a level in our appreciation which was comparable to that of the Impressionists. Our three children all studied for a time with Arthur Lismer at the Montreal Museum of Fine Arts. It was only later that we really understood what a privilege they had had.

Another delay, indeed a failure, of appreciation, has dogged me for half a century. I became pediatrician to the son and twin daughters of Sam Borenstein – whom I actually met in the taxi which he was driving in order to make ends meet – and in retrospect I should have asked for a painting in lieu of fees.

I also became friendly with Norman Leibovitch, whose wife, Pearl, was a social work colleague and valued friend of Sheila's. After his death, a score of his paintings hung for some time in the ground-floor corridors of the Montreal Children's Hospital.

Art entered our lives more directly when my aunt Ellen Ballon, the concert pianist, established a close friendship with the sculptor Sally Ryan, called Tammy by those close to her. Tammy had studied with Jacob Epstein and become recognized in her own right. She did a bust of my father which was a sensitive capture of his thoughtfulness and his wisdom. She was the granddaughter of Thomas Fortune Ryan, who held his son, her father, in low esteem and so left his substantial wealth entirely to her. The relation with Ellen and with our family lasted for many years, until Tammy's untimely death from cancer.

Ellen also died of cancer, several years later. One day we learned that some months before her death, she had sat for a portrait by a British artist named Suzanne Beadle. Ellen had not liked the painting – it is a faithful and expressive likeness, but perhaps she felt that it revealed the earliest signs of her developing illness – and so it had remained in Suzanne Beadle's studio. I had occasion to go to London. I went to see the portrait, liked it a great deal, and readily assented to the very reasonable price which the artist set.

A few years earlier, I had been in Israel and had been taken for an evening to a beachfront square in the old city of Jaffa. My host had asked me what I was interested in seeing, and I chose art. I found myself in front of a gallery owned by a Frenchman named Jean Tiroche, and I went in to browse. The main room was jammed with undistinguished local works, but at the back a door opened into a smaller space which had paintings of much greater interest and value. I saw a Raoul Dufy and an Armand Guillaumin, and I turned a corner – and found myself staring at a portrait, by Manè-Katz, of a young Aunt Ellen seated at the keyboard. I would very much have liked to acquire it, but the asking price of $25,000 was far beyond my means.

My interest in art has remained undimmed and indeed has expanded, although with a few exceptions – Édouard Vuillard's interiors, for example – I remain in arrested appreciation of the era of the French Impressionists. I have made honest efforts to understand non-representational art, but it does not reach me. I recognize that with the advent of photography, painting and sculpture were no longer the only means of recording history and providing portraits of its protagonists – or visually telling stories, or illustrating religion, or recording daily life. But I respond to representation – impressionistic, by all means – and am lost without it.

I have always been particularly drawn to portraits: Memling, Holbein, John Singer Sargent, and very particularly Sir Henry Raeburn, for whom Sheila and I made a pilgrimage to Edinburgh and Glasgow a few years ago.

I have twice been a subject myself. My friend Eva Oppenheimer Prager, whose son was my patient, painted my portrait. And during my years as Commissioner of Official Languages, I was introduced to a Canadian sculptor named Sandra Shaw, and sat for a portrait bust. I was, and am, unashamedly pleased with the result.

# A Professional Career, 1940–1966

## LEARNING TO BE A PEDIATRICIAN

In the summer of 1940 – university holidays were over four months long – I got a job as an unpaid assistant laboratory technician at the Children's Hospital in Montreal. I learned basic urinalysis and was initiated into the recognition of normal and abnormal blood cells under the microscope. The technician, the pint-sized Alfred Hewitt, welcomed me warmly, and so did all the other members of the hospital family. The following year I was back again, working in the more sophisticated hematology laboratory. One day the technician, the personable and competent Jean Macfarlane, received the devastating news that her brother had been killed overseas, and all of a sudden I was in charge, responsible for providing diagnoses to the resident and attending staff physicians.

When I became a medical student, my father began to offer an hour or more during the weekend when he would take me and two or three classmates around the wards and teach us about pediatric illnesses. Diagnostic tools were limited compared to those of the present day, and the understanding of what was happening in a child's body depended on clinical acumen, a talent with which he was outstandingly endowed. Although I was still captivated with journalism, I was attracted to pediatrics.

In medical school, no doubt because of my summer jobs, I was drawn towards laboratory medicine and particularly hematology. In my oral examination in pathology, however, I came before the hematologist-in-chief and stumbled badly, and I did not have the nerve subsequently to ask him for a job. My father said, "Why don't you come to the Children's for a year and figure out what you want to do?" With a sense of *faute de mieux*, I agreed.

On my first morning I walked onto the older children's ward, and my life changed. The head nurse, an intimidating skipper-next-to-God person (who in her retirement would become a mellow correspondent) for whom I had always been an assistant, interim laboratory technician, greeted me with deference, brought me to the bedside of a recently admitted patient, showed me the child's chart, which had been written up by a departing resident, and said, "Dr Goldbloom, what are your orders?" I managed to maintain a composure I did not feel, dig down into my rudimentary medical-school knowledge, and come up with an answer – and I was hooked.

Life as an intern, of course, had its ups and downs, but it was a great experience. In medical school I had had only a year and a half of clinical contact with patients (it begins much earlier nowadays) and none at all with their families. I discovered a talent for the latter, with an ability to translate science and pathology into laypersons' language. That became and remained a major gratification in pediatric practice.

The Children's had a main building, reached by a fairly steep winding road up from Cedar Avenue, and four detached pavilions out behind it. The smallest had ten beds devoted to infectious diseases – tuberculosis, salmonella infections (including typhoid fever), meningococcal and other types of meningitis, etc. – and it was the only depressing part of the hospital because each child was isolated in a cubicle and, before antibiotics, many of these diseases were untreatable and unstoppable. Antibiotics began to arrive, however – first the sulpha drugs, then penicillin (which we injected in tiny

5,000- and 10,000-unit doses), then streptomycin (which had the significant hazard of sometimes damaging hearing) – and unimagined positive outcomes became possible.

Another pavilion, three times the size, was devoted to rheumatic fever. This was a disquietingly frequent disease, and we puzzled over its causation. (When we discovered that it was a complication of streptococcal infection, we learned that adequate treatment with penicillin would prevent it, and it has essentially disappeared.) Rheumatic fever could seriously damage the heart, and this indeed had happened to some of the children on that ward. Others, however, had suffered no harm, but were routinely prescribed bed rest for several weeks. One would walk into the ward and find "bed rest" children jumping up and down, turning somersaults, and climbing over the sides of the beds. When my father became pediatrician-in-chief, he further enhanced his reputation and elated dozens of families by "throwing" these children out of the hospital.

Poliomyelitis was a dreaded disease. There were cases every summer, and they would build up to a major epidemic every fifteen years: 1916, 1931, 1946. The 1961 epidemic, however, did not take place because Dr Jonas Salk had devised a vaccine. Treatment was limited to re-strengthening weakened muscles. A few children had their breathing function affected and needed an "iron lung" respirator, from which they rarely emerged. Each summer one of the outside wards would be converted to a polio pavilion, and it was not the happiest of places.

An Australian nurse, Sister Elizabeth Kenny, had convinced herself and others that the application of hot packs to affected muscles would restore their strength. Since paralysis was not due to damage in the muscle itself, but to the destructive effect of the virus in the spinal nerves, her well-meaning approach could not be effective. But she had a widespread quasi-religious following, and my father was one of those who had the ungrateful task of telling the public the truth.

Although grave outcomes have always, at least in modern times, been far less frequent in pediatric hospitals than in others, we coped with some untreatable and irreversible diseases. One was leukemia; another was tuberculous meningitis. Supporting parents and siblings and grandparents through such ordeals was something we had to learn to do. It challenged our humanity.

There was a lighter side to our internship experience when, at least once a year, we held the Beer and Oyster Party. The resident staff would write and perform a musical play lampooning the attending staff, and my theatrical experience and operatic avocation were put to good use.

After two years at the Children's, my father urged me to gain experience in another setting. In his postgraduate training he had spent two years at the Babies' Hospital in New York, and that was where I went. The pediatrician-in-chief, Rustin McIntosh, was warm and intelligent, and several members of the attending staff were leading-edge contributors to the advancement of knowledge. One whom I admired especially was Virginia Apgar, like my wife, Sheila, a graduate of Mount Holyoke College in Massachusetts, who conceived the Apgar Index for assessing difficulties that infants might experience immediately after birth.

My first attending staff mentor was Fred Silverman, a radiologist who was a fun person and an astute clinical observer; we gravitated into a lasting friendship. My second was Bill Silverman (no relation), who became a world expert and a seminal researcher in the care of the newborn. One of the luminaries was "Cactus Jack" Caffey, the radiologist-in-chief – crusty but caring and generous with his teaching. He called us in one day and showed us x-rays of an infant with multiple fractures. None of us made the diagnosis. It was the first case of child abuse I had ever seen.

Babies' Hospital was not, however, a uniformly happy experience. It was much more focused on research than the Montreal Children's, and this was the driving force that often determined how children were looked after. Accumulating numbers of a particular problem in order to build a statistically significant cohort for publication was a dominant preoccupation. I fell afoul of this obsession on more than one occasion.

Newborn infants, especially boys, are sometimes afflicted by a condition called pyloric stenosis. The valve at the farther outlet of the stomach, the pylorus, becomes thickened and blocks up, preventing milk from going through and causing projectile vomiting. A simple operation to split the thickened muscle is immediately effective. The Babies' had a special six-crib unit for these infants. One Friday we found ourselves with twelve pyloric stenosis patients, all vomiting everything and all dehydrated to varying degrees. The surgeon-in-chief was going away for the weekend, and he ordered us to keep these infants going with intravenous hydration until he got back on Monday, refusing to allow any other surgeon to operate, so that he could build his personal statistics.

On another weekend I got into trouble with the great Hattie Alexander, a brilliant microbiologist who elucidated the behaviour of different bacteria. She had received special permission from the New York Department of Health to have infants with pertussis (whooping cough), normally sent to an infectious disease hospital, admitted to the Babies'. One Friday night one of the infants became rather severely ill, and it was evident that she had developed pneumonia notwithstanding the anti-pertussis antibiotic she was receiving. I judged it advisable to add penicillin, which was considered to have no effect on the whooping cough germ. When Hattie arrived on Monday morning, she was incensed and brought me before a meeting of the staff because I had, in her view, made this child ineligible for inclusion in her study.

Patients were, of course, referred to the Babies' by outside physicians, generally family doctors, who were designated by the uncomplimentary term L M D s (L for Local). I was uncomfortable with that disdain and with other aspects of the hospital's philosophy. When Rustin McIntosh offered me a further six months of residency, I thanked him and headed back to the clinically focused milieu of Montreal.

## STARTING A PRACTICE

I began, naturally enough, as my father's assistant. He would ask me to do a house call on an evening or during a weekend, and I felt that my training gave me confidence in making a diagnosis and choosing a treatment. Parents seemed to trust my judgment. It was an enjoyable experience. My father, who was generally regarded as God by his patients, loved to tell of an incident that occurred early on, as I was beginning to become known. (I had the family name, which was an asset, but he was the *real* Doctor Goldbloom.) The phone rang when he was alone in the office, and he answered it. A lady asked, in French, "Docteur Goldbloom?" He said yes. "Le père ou le fils?" (The father or the son?), she queried. He responded, "C'est le Saint Esprit" (I'm the Holy Spirit). She was not amused.

Some years before, my parents had sold our house on Crescent Street, and my father had taken an office in the Medical Arts Building at the corner of Guy and Sherbrooke streets. A small room there became my consulting room. A number of obstetricians, not only among my contemporaries but of my father's generation as well, referred newborns to me. By my second year, I was becoming quite busy.

My French was not yet fully fluent, but it was serviceable enough for pediatric purposes, and my francophone practice grew quite quickly. That my father was so well-known obviously helped. Many of my pediatric colleagues, especially those who were somewhat older, placed geographic limits on their practices. "I don't go east of Saint Denis Street," said more than one. I went all over the city and into all but the farthest suburbs, and the word of my availability spread.

When I returned from New York City in January 1949, my father told me that he had been instrumental in something rather momentous: the amalgamation of the two associations of pediatricians, one French-speaking and the other English-speaking, into a single Association of Pediatricians of the Province of Quebec. He asked me to become a member and to work for the organization's success. I was a faithful attendee at meetings and spoke French as often as I spoke English. The communities discovered each other, and the association flourished.

Pediatrics was still a very young specialty. In 1949 less than thirty years had passed since my father had opened his pioneering office, and it was just twelve years since Pediatrics had become autonomous at McGill. There was much debate about the role of the pediatrician: should he (or, increasingly, she) aim to be the primary-care physician for all children or essentially a consultant to family physicians fulfilling that function? The debate remained unresolved – there were not enough pediatricians for the former role and too many for the latter. Statistics at that time showed that 11 per cent of Canadian children were in the care of pediatricians, 75 per cent in that of family physicians – and 14 per cent in the care of no one, a troubling figure. The Association of Pediatricians had no lack of material for its ongoing agenda.

By this time my own practice was booming. Children came to the office for checkups and minor conditions; more significant problems were seen at home. House calls were enjoyable, not only because I liked driving, even in a snowstorm, but, more importantly, because I gained a sense of the home circumstances, and of the family constellation in which the child lived. Some of the poorest homes were the most spotlessly clean. Often the house calls were numerous and kept me out until late in the evening, but parents were always pleased to see me and often offered me nourishment. I was always formal with the parents of my patients, but that did not preclude many warm (and lasting) relationships.

Among my most treasured professional relationships were with luminaries of the French-language theatre, notably Huguette Oligny and her brother-in-law Jean-Louis Roux. Jean Gascon and Mia Riddez also had me look after their children. I had wonderful conversations with Doris Lussier ("Le Père

Gédéon"). One day Gratien Gélinas brought me his daughter Mitsou. Guy Hoffman called me early one morning to see his daughter Roseline. And one day a Mrs Watier arrived with her daughter Lise.

A rather special experience was a request for a house call from André Laurendeau, publisher of *Le Devoir*. It was said that in earlier times he had expressed negative views about people of my religion, but before I left his house – the problem had not been serious, and for once I was not under pressure – we had a prolonged and cordial conversation.

I became pediatrician to the family of Ed Roebuck. Ed was a right-handed pitcher for the Montreal Royals, and he did well enough to earn promotion to the parent Dodgers. He and his wife, a charming former airline stewardess, were pleasantly surprised to have a doctor who knew so much about baseball.

Routine checkups for healthy children – for example, to fill out forms for summer camps – were considered boring by many of my colleagues. I obviously found intellectual stimulation in the challenge of a serious or complicated disease, but I did not wish for them, and I thanked God every time I examined a healthy child.

Immunizations were an important part of pediatric practice. I saw two cases of diphtheria, none of tetanus, and none of smallpox, because a vaccine against each was in general use. The vaccine against whooping cough, by contrast, was not 100 per cent effective, but what cases there were were milder and became rare in infancy, when the disease was often fatal. Poliomyelitis virtually disappeared. Vaccines against measles, German measles, and mumps came along a little later. These were very significant achievements, and it is unfortunate that some people, few in percentage but nevertheless significant in number, believe that vaccines are dangerous and that it is better to get the "natural" disease. They do not appreciate how favourably the face of pediatrics has changed by virtue of almost universal immunization in developed countries (and increasingly in others).

In all my years of practice I saw only one child with autism. I cannot agree with those who insist that there has been no increase in the incidence of the disease, that we simply are better at diagnosing it. One might have called it something else, but one could not have failed to recognize that something serious was going on, and in retrospect to realize that it was autism. The idea that vaccines, in particular the one against measles, German measles, and mumps, could cause autism, became a source of anxiety for parents in the early years of this century. It has now been concluded that vaccines do not induce autism, but the concern has caused rates of immunization to fall in Canada. As a result, grave diseases such as poliomyelitis, which vaccines had eliminated from this country and from much of the world, are at risk of reappearing. Because we no longer see the disease and its crippling and sometimes fatal effects, we are no longer afraid of it – and no longer understand the importance, for the whole of society, of maintaining our children's immunization against it.

I tried to get across to parents that risks from vaccines are infinitesimal, while the risks from polio are very serious indeed. Vaccines do not overwhelm the immune system. There are germs all around us, and every day our immune system is hit by thousands of them. Vaccines are treated so that the germs in them are harmless, but still able to stimulate immunity. Only by immunizing virtually all children can we protect against epidemics and fatalities.

In my experience, senior physicians were, by and large, remarkably welcoming, treating younger colleagues almost as equals. One of whom I was in awe was Wilder Penfield, the great neurosurgeon who had been the founding head of the Montreal Neurological Institute. One day I referred a patient to him. This was a young man of seventeen, whose mother, a widow, was a friend and neighbour of my mother-in-law in New York. He had intractable epilepsy, with several major seizures every day. She had consulted neurosurgeons in Boston and New York and Philadelphia, and all had recommended a radical operation, the removal of the entire cerebral cortex on the side of the brain on which the seizures were originating. She had heard of Dr Penfield, and she wanted his opinion.

He came to the same conclusion, and she decided to trust him. The day before the operation, he convened a "case conference," which he invited me to attend. There were some thirty people present – neurosurgeons, neurologists, nurses, social workers – and he invited each one to speak and to comment on the advisability of the radical procedure. A good many did, and almost all were negative, saying that the mother was overprotective and could do a better job of managing the problem. Dr Penfield listened attentively, and finally he spoke. He said one sentence: "Not one of you has ever spent twenty-four consecutive hours looking after a person with intractable epilepsy." And he did the operation, with success.

When I was first in practice, exposure to a pollutant was not something that pediatricians and other physicians considered in the differential diagnosis of diseases. That would emerge as a major educational responsibility for me after I became Minister of the Environment in 1970. Determining the relation between disease and the presence of a chemical substance in the environment – lead in gasoline was a conspicuous example, and there is much less lead in children's bodies since its elimination – was a great contribution to public health. Health care professionals needed to learn a new way of thinking.

I had enjoyed practising pediatrics, and it was neither boredom nor burnout that impelled me to enter public life. Even when I became a minister, I maintained an office and practised on weekends and during the legislature's recess periods. I stopped, however, taking on newborn babies, who needed a pediatrician close at hand and not some 270 kilometres away. I found myself becoming a specialist in adolescence, and of course, as my patients became adults, they moved on to adult physicians. In 1981, a short time after I had resigned from the Quebec legislature, I gave up practice.

### RAISING A FAMILY

The practice of pediatrics in the house-call era, with its ninety-hour weeks and its unpredictable demands, complicated family life, but with Sheila's extraordinary abilities, we worked things out. Sheila had arrived in Montreal in January 1949. It was a culture shock, not only in terms of languages but also because she had to adapt to a very different kind of community, more conservative, more close-knit, and more demanding of its members. Most people were welcoming, but integration did not come automatically.

She set about finding a job. She had been on the staff of the League of Women Voters of New York State and had led a group at the Ethical Culture Society, so she was already focused on community organization. Her first approaches were in the Jewish community, but there were no openings. By chance, she heard of a receptionist position at the YWCA, and when she applied, the executive director looked at her qualifications and offered her the job of director of the Young Adult Department. It was the first time that a non-Christian had joined the program staff.

Our daughter, Susan, was born in November 1950. She was agile, climbing a jungle gym at twelve months of age, and a quick learner. I read to her a good deal; her favourite was *Woody Woodpecker*, and when Sheila brought son Michael home in January 1953, we had practised while she was at the hospital, and Susan was able to finish sentences throughout the book. She started at Weston School, just up the hill from our house on Grove Park, moved to Saint George's, and then went to Dana Hall in Wellesley, Massachusetts, for eleventh and twelfth grades. When it came time for university applications, we naturally gave particular consideration to Sheila's alma mater, Mount Holyoke, in South Hadley, Massachusetts. Dana Hall's college adviser, however, although a Mount Holyoke graduate herself, urged Susan to apply to Harvard (Radcliffe for women in those days), and she was accepted.

I had begun with Susan a tradition that I maintained with her two brothers. I set a week aside, and she and I got in the car and visited eight or nine universities in Canada and the United States, having an interview at each. She made six applications, with a "dream school" at the top of the list and a "fall-back school" at the bottom, and the responses were mostly positive, giving her the luxury of choice.

Many university students at that time took a junior year abroad, but Susan opted for an internship in the city administration of New York. A wide range of positions was available, and she chose the Budget Office, which could have been dry and mathematical but turned out to have an intellectually stimulating involvement in a broad range of social issues for which financing had to be carefully analyzed. After graduation she went into the banking field, and a good many years later she made a deeply felt decision to leave and co-found Knowledge in the Public Interest, offering policy and administrative consulting services to non-profit organizations and even governments in the field of education, among others. As the eldest, Susan has been a trailblazer for her brothers. She has inherited her mother's ability to listen with genuine and constructive empathy and to advise with compassion and insight.

Michael went to Selwyn House, to Williston Academy in Easthampton, Massachusetts, and then to Harvard. He graduated in law from McGill and joined Martineau Walker, where he specialized in the labour field. After a number of years he opted for a change of careers, becoming head of the Montreal YMCA and guiding that historic organization through a financial minefield. But his real love was journalism, and he spent seven years as publisher of *The Gazette*, Montreal's English-language daily. He was involved for a time in McGill's Institute for the Study of Canada and was then tapped to become publisher of the *Toronto Star*, Canada's largest newspaper. When that stint ended, he came back to McGill as a vice-principal and was then made head of Bishop's University in Lennoxville (Sherbrooke), Quebec, where he turned around a difficult situation, increased enrolment, raised the institution's profile and reputation, and drew widespread plaudits.

Michael fulfilled my early ambitions in journalism, and he has been a respected and effective participant in the ongoing negotiation of a modus vivendi between francophones and anglophones in a Quebec which both can help to make flourish. After university, he had spent a year in Paris at the Institut d'études politiques, the "Sciences Po." While there, he met a young woman who was a committed Communist and with whom he made a group trip to the Soviet Union. We, Sheila in particular, were concerned that this association might develop into a lasting relationship, and we decided that I should go to Paris and assess the situation. I confided in Premier Robert Bourassa that I was going and why (I was then in government), and asked him to keep it confidential. I made the trip, took Michael and his friend for a gourmet dinner, and felt that he had to, at his age, work things out for himself. On my return I was in the ministers' dining room of the parliamentary restaurant, and Robert came in, clapped me on the shoulder, and said in a loud voice before about thirty people, "So, how is the Left in France?" I could have throttled him.

Michael has a talent for names. It was he who suggested that of Alliance Quebec, it was he who proposed naming the English-speaking community's child and youth welfare agency in honour of Manny Batshaw, and it was he who tagged me with the politically incorrect sobriquet that my grandchildren use, "Papa Doc."

Our second son, Jonathan, arrived in October 1955. He also attended Selwyn House, went to Milton Academy south of Boston, and followed his siblings to Harvard. He got a degree in Canadian Studies from Carleton University in Ottawa and an MBA from the University of Western Ontario in London. After five years as executive assistant to Michael Warren, the head of Canada's Post Office, he then developed a computerized program for the home delivery of groceries and subsequently joined the Columbia Group, the business founded by his wife, Alice Switocz.

Their small enterprise was eventually sold to a major company, Cossette, and Jonathan served there for four years as a vice-president. He then launched his own firm, with notable success both in business terms and in community endeavours. He directed Bob Rae's campaigns for the leadership of the Liberal Party of Canada, he was instrumental in keeping the Shriners' Hospital in Montreal, and he played a major role in obtaining for psychologists the right to diagnose and treat children with autism.

Jonathan has a conspicuous, infectious, and unique laugh and a constructively challenging attitude about life. He has inherited my love of the theatre, but not my singing voice. At Milton he was cast as the catcher in *Damn Yankees*, but the script had to be changed so that he asked someone else to sing "You Gotta Have Heart." But his (inherited) passion for the theatre is such that he was named to the board of the Stratford Shakespearean Festival.

Despite the demands of pediatric practice, I had close relationships with the children. Coming home generally late at night, I would go into each of their bedrooms and was often rewarded by a brief waking-up and a bit of conversation. I was a resource for their homework, particularly when Michael and Jonathan were required by Selwyn House to produce essays over the weekend. We worked on them together, wrestling with the dilemma of whether the boys should simply submit what they had written or whether I should be their editor. We opted for the latter role, and in retrospect they felt – Michael in particular in his newspaper career – that I had significantly honed their writing skills.

Sports were important to both boys, and Susan took up dance. I managed to attend her performances and to spend time throwing a baseball back and forth across Grove Park with Michael and Jonathan. I wanted to be an involved, not an absentee, father. We had family lunches on Sundays, often with invited guests. We took family holidays in the summer and sometimes skiing trips in the winter. In one of my election campaigns, Jonathan accompanied me all over the province.

Because the boys shared my interest in baseball, we became collectors of baseball cards. We built up a substantial collection, and rather than keep them in a box, we decided to display them on shirt cardboards. I very carefully taped them on, and we all admired the results – until we found that the taping had made them unsaleable and we had sacrificed a small fortune.

After Jonathan started to attend school all day, Sheila decided to pursue a master's degree in social work. McGill allowed her to do so on a part-time basis, spreading the three-year program over five. Immediately upon graduation, she went to consult the director of the school, Dr John J.O. Moore, about career possibilities, and he offered her a position on the faculty. She taught for thirty years, and even after retirement, she continued to be academically involved, working with the teachers who supervise social work students in their field placements.

One of Sheila's School of Social Work colleagues, Jim Torczyner, established the McGill Middle East Program in Civil Society and Peace-Building (now called ICAN), bringing together Israeli, Jordanian, and Palestinian students. Each is assigned a tutor, and Sheila became mentor successively to three young women: Amal, a Bedouin from the Negev, Najwa, a Palestinian from Ramallah, and Samar, a Jordanian from Amman. Each developed an especially warm relationship with her and secondarily with me, and we have remained in sustained and affectionate contact with them. They make us feel that peace is possible.

Sheila plays a unique role as a trusted adviser to successive family generations and to friends and colleagues. She has an instinct for balancing the professional and the personal and for making light appear at the end of the tunnel. She nourishes friendships and inspires loyalties. In 2011 she was co-chairperson (with the Minister for Seniors, Marguerite Blais, and Dr Réjean Hébert, who was subsequently elected to the Quebec legislature and became Minister of Health and Minister for Seniors as well) of a Quebec government commission that went all over the province to hold hearings on the living conditions of senior citizens.

Sheila and I have been mutually supportive in our community involvements, which have been numerous. She was a stalwart of the Jewish Junior Welfare League, served on the board of Centraide, headed the Red Feather Foundation and managed its merger into the Foundation of Greater Montreal, chaired the board of Vanier College, evaluated schools with the Canadian Educational Standards Institute, and for thirty years cooked for a Meals on Wheels program at a nearby church. We both have been honoured with the Order of Canada and the Ordre national du Québec. But our greatest reward has been to see our children become talented and socially responsible adults and to admire how they and their spouses have raised the next generation. We are proud of their achievements and grateful for their affection for us and for each other.

# Public Life, 1966–1979

Although I may have been a touch more interested in politics than the average person, my ninety-hour weeks as a pediatrician kept that interest remote. It occasionally crossed my mind in the early 1960s that Alan Macnaughton had represented Mount Royal riding for a long time and that a day would come when he would step aside, but there was no germ of a strategic plan to fill that vacancy. Pediatrics was my foreseeable future.

My political career began, unbeknownst to me, one afternoon in 1958 in the auditorium of Sainte-Justine Hospital. The Association of Pediatricians of the Province of Quebec (APPQ) was holding a regular meeting, and a major item on the agenda was the coverage of pediatric care by insurance companies, notably Blue Cross–Blue Shield and Les Services de Santé du Québec. That coverage was frustratingly limited, and the discussion revolved around possibilities for improving it. After a good deal of revolving, I offered the opinion that these problems were going to be with us for a long time and that we should establish a standing committee to deal with them. Heads nodded, a resolution was unanimously adopted, and as the initiator of the idea, I was named chairman.

"Medical economics" was the usual name for such committees, and it impelled us to take a broad approach to our mandate. We involved colleagues from different parts of the province and discovered a strong desire for a fee schedule, which we proceeded to produce. We came to understand that insurance companies did not cover pediatric care because it was largely preventive and predictable, and therefore not insurable in the true sense: that is, charging everyone a small premium to cover the costs of an illness that would affect only a few people in any given year. Universal, publicly funded health insurance was vaguely on the horizon, so it was in our more distant thoughts, but it was not until the 1960s that it became a front-and-centre issue.

Our committee's report to the A P P Q 's annual meeting was well received, and we were encouraged to keep working. At the A G M a year later, the president, Dr Jessie Boyd Scriver, asked me to come down before the meeting started and talk with the guest speaker, Dr T. James Quintin of Sherbrooke, a distinguished internist, who had led a Canadian Medical Association team to Australia to learn about the national health insurance system there. He told me that Dr Scriver had said complimentary things about what I had been doing, and he asked me to take on the Medical Economics Committee of the Quebec Medical Association.

The Q M A was headed at that time by another physician from Sherbrooke, the radiologist René Duberger. The vice-president was a Montreal surgeon, an Acadian from Nova Scotia named Normand Belliveau, and the executive director was a layman, Jean-Marc Denault. They welcomed me with open arms, deciding that Duberger would be Athos; Denault, Porthos; Belliveau, Aramis; and I, D'Artagnan. René Duberger felt strongly that the Q M A was too Montreal-centred and was unknown and unappreciated in other parts of the province. So I found myself sent out to places such as Rivière-du-Loup, Rimouski, Rouyn-Noranda, and Saint-Georges-de-Beauce, making speeches in French and dialoguing with physicians and occasionally journalists. Duberger was right: such visits, virtually unprecedented, were deeply appreciated.

In 1961 the federal government created a commission headed by Mr Justice L. Emmett Hall of Saskatchewan (born in Saint-Colomban, Quebec), to hold hearings all across Canada and recommend a publicly funded health care system. As chairperson of the QMA's Medical Economics Committee, I became the principal author and lead presenter of the organization's brief. In preparation, I was sent to sit in on the commission's hearings in Fredericton, Halifax, and several other cities. Our appearance was one of the last, and our brief was well received, notably because we concluded with a commitment to the democratic process, rather than an automatic opposition to change.

The board of the Quebec College of Physicians and Surgeons was up for election in 1962, and I was urged to run. My opponent was Dr Joachim Brabander, a senior physician at the Royal Victoria Hospital, better known and more experienced, but I came out on top. I found myself one of twenty-one governors, the only English-speaking member except for the (unilingual) representative of McGill, and I was elected third vice-president.

We had all-day, two-day meetings, conducted entirely in French. I managed, but was far from perfect. A colleague, Jacques Boulay, a hematologist from Quebec City who was also newly elected, spontaneously took on a very special responsibility. At the end of each day he would come over with a notebook in which he had recorded all the mistakes I had made in French and teach me to correct them. He would go so far as to explain the nuances between different words and phrases and the subtleties of sentence structure. I owe him an enormous debt.

The president of the College was Dr Jean-Baptiste Jobin, a person of great wisdom who had served for eight years as dean of Medicine at Université Laval. One day he said to us, "Publicly funded, universal health care insurance is coming. We have two choices. We can oppose it until it is inevitably imposed on us, or we can become active participants in the debate and help shape the system." We chose the latter course and embarked on a series of meetings with labour unions and with other organizations. It was thus that I met Jean Marchand, who headed the Confederation of National Trade Unions (CNTU / CSN), Marcel Pépin, who later succeeded him, Louis Laberge, of the Quebec Federation of Labour, and René Lévesque.

In the summer of 1962, four months before I was elected to the College, Premier Jean Lesage had brought in a bill called the Hospitals Act. Quebec at that time had some 250 hospitals, about 100 of them well-recognized institutions and the others mostly small private establishments. These latter were of very variable quality, and Premier Lesage, as part of the Quiet Revolution, wanted to implement uniform standards for patient safety and quality of care. Indeed, some hair-raising deficiencies and dangers had come to light: hospitals in which the patient's chart contained no record of what surgery had been done, what had been found at the operation, what the tissue removed had revealed; where the nurses recorded no account of the patient's hour-to-hour and day-to-day condition; where the rooms adjacent to the x-ray department were not shielded from radiation; where medications were not adequately refrigerated; and so on.

The Hospitals Act was of the type called enabling legislation, setting out general principles that would be elaborated by detailed regulations to be adopted by order-in-council, that is, by cabinet decree. Physicians and hospital administrators had reacted strongly, insisting that it was up to professionals like themselves rather than to bureaucrats to produce such regulations. To everyone's surprise, Lesage agreed. The act was amended so that the College and the two hospital associations, the Association of Hospitals of Quebec and the Association of Catholic Hospitals of Quebec (the two later amalgamated), would write the regulations. We created a task force.

Unfortunately, the work did not go well. Our task force did not communicate effectively with the hospital associations, progress was snail-like, and after two years Premier Lesage lost patience. Dr Jobin and the three vice-presidents made a pilgrimage to Quebec City – the first time I had ever set foot in the legislative building. We made the rounds of several ministers, including Eric Kierans and René Lévesque, and they went to bat for us with the premier. He relented.

A year later we still did not have a document. Lesage again put forward legislation to take the regulations out of our hands. We made a similar pilgrimage, but this time we did not succeed. We met with the premier himself, however, and he offered us a deal, one last chance. He said he would have the bill passed by the lower house, but would then wait exactly twelve days before sending it to the upper house, which still existed at that time. (It was abolished in 1969.) We headed home with determination to succeed.

We promptly dissolved our task force. We charged our president, Dr Jobin, and our first vice-president, Dr Georges Lachaîne, a Verdun cardiologist for whom I had great esteem, with sitting down with the heads of the two hospital associations and not leaving the motel room until they had a set of regulations. On the eleventh day they emerged with a document. We sent a telegram to Lesage, asking for a meeting. He gave us an appointment. It turned out to be on a beautiful August Friday afternoon.

The premier received us cordially, took the thick document, and said to us that he obviously did not have the professional competence to evaluate it himself. As we sat there, he picked up the telephone and called one of the associate deputy ministers of health. He requested a report by the Monday morning. The A D M had planned a weekend in the country with his family, and he was not, as the British say, best pleased. On the Monday morning he brought in a nitpicking negative report, and our document was rejected.

I felt that I was at a major crossroads in my life. Either I set aside public responsibility and devoted myself solely to the practice of pediatrics, or I recognized that I was not where decisions that could have broad and profound impact on people's lives were really taken – and I should try to get there. My four years on the board of the College had brought me from a role of helping people individually to one of considering policies to benefit the population at large. I was ready for the move.

## THE COMPLICATED PATH

I set my sights on the provincial legislature, but I had no idea how to proceed. François Zalloni, the director of communications at the College of Physicians and Surgeons, was a former journalist, and I was aware that he knew a good many people in public life. I confided in him, and he reacted positively and offered to test the waters on my behalf. Zalloni took the train to Quebec City, spoke confidentially with several ministers, and came back with an encouraging response.

On the train coming back he ran into Jean Marchand. They chatted animatedly, and Marchand asked him what had brought him to Quebec City. Zalloni was hesitant, but under pressure he told Marchand about my possible candidacy. Marchand, remembering me from our constructive conversations about medicare, said, "Ask him to call me." He invited me to breakfast the following Thursday at the old Mount Royal Hotel.

Marchand told me, "Everyone knows that when I resigned as general secretary of the Confederation of National Trade Unions, it was to go into federal politics. No announcement has been made as yet, and that is because I told Prime Minister Lester Pearson that I would not go alone; that I would run only if I could bring with me a team of people rooted in Quebec and committed to Canada. So far, the people I have recruited are all French Canadians, and I am looking for candidates from other backgrounds. Will you join me?"

My head was spinning. I resisted the temptation to say yes on the spot, and asked for three days to think it over. I talked with my family and with two close friends, Mel Rothman and Fred Kaufman, and called Jean to accept. He sent me to see the chief organizer for Quebec, Louis de Gonzague (Bob) Giguère, later a senator. Giguère was cordial but noncommittal, and said I would have to see Guy Favreau, Lester Pearson's Quebec lieutenant, and Senator Maurice Lamontagne. After some time, I was called and directed to a room on the top floor of the Windsor Hotel for 1:30 on a Tuesday afternoon.

I was kept cooling my heels for half an hour in the corridor, and finally the door opened and I was invited in. A third person was in the room, and I recognized the well-respected newspaper editor Gérard Pelletier. The three had obviously been having a long lunch, and the mood was jovial. I was, of course, tense, but I was excited by the prospect of, for the very first time in my life, being where affairs of state were seriously and thoughtfully discussed. They continued their conversation for some minutes as if I was not there, and it turned out that they were reminiscing about their days as *collège classique* boarding students, the troubles they got into, and the tricks they played on their teachers.

After a while, Pelletier left. Favreau and Lamontagne invited me to talk about myself, asked a few questions, and said thank you and goodbye. It came, then, as no surprise when, some time later, Marchand announced his intention to run and identified Pelletier as a teammate. Pierre Elliott Trudeau, about whom I knew next to nothing, was also named. I was not. Marchand called to say that things were progressing and were in the hands of the "organizers." I waited.

Liberal candidates were being selected in riding after riding. Marchand was slotted without difficulty into a riding in Quebec City. One was found for Pelletier in east-end Montreal – or, rather, created by twisting the arm of the veteran incumbent to step aside. (He was subsequently named a judge and was extremely happy.) Trudeau found no takers.

The calling of the election had engendered a rather extraordinary problem. With the publication of the 1961 census results, demographic shifts had to be taken into account and a new electoral map drawn. That had been done, and the map had been made public, but there was an interval before it took effect, and in that interval the election was called. That meant that the election would be based on the old map.

Back in 1911 Prime Minister Sir Wilfrid Laurier had made a commitment to the Jewish community of Montreal that the Liberal Party of Canada would always present a Jewish candidate in one of the Montreal ridings. The designated riding was Cartier, covering the historic immigrant staging area adjacent to St Lawrence Boulevard. But in the new electoral map, Cartier was to disappear. In the years since 1911 the Jewish community had grown and had progressively moved westward. It was now concentrated in the riding of Mount Royal. It was evident that Mount Royal should replace Cartier as the "Jewish seat," and Milton Klein, the MP for Cartier, asked to be permitted to run in Mount Royal. His request was refused.

As Liberal candidates were chosen in riding after riding, it began to dawn on perceptive observers that the organizers wanted to run Trudeau in Mount Royal. If that were the case, the Laurier promise would be broken the next time around, because Cartier would meanwhile have disappeared. Senator Lazarus Phillips, a distinguished lawyer and the senior Jewish Liberal in Quebec, reacted vigorously. I waited, in limbo, in the wings.

Fourteen days before the deadline, a nominating convention was announced for Mount Royal riding – but no candidates. At about noon on the following day, a Friday, I received a call authorizing me to put forward my candidacy. Two days later they told Trudeau to do the same. Marchand was furious and felt that both he and Prime Minister Pearson had been betrayed, but there was essentially no room for manoeuvre.

On receiving the green light, I called a good friend, Jean-Pierre Côté, whose eight children had been my patients. He was a Pearson minister and later became a senator and then lieutenant-governor of Quebec. He came over immediately from his home in Longueuil, and we made the rounds of the newspapers and the principal radio and television stations to announce my intentions.

Pierre Elliott Trudeau and I met for the first time at the first all-candidates meeting. Other hats had been thrown in the ring: Monty Berger, an experienced public relations executive and a friend; Sophie Crestohl, whose husband had represented Cartier until his untimely death (Milton Klein had succeeded him); and Stuart Smith, an academic who later became leader of the Liberal Party of Ontario. There was instantaneous positive chemistry between Pierre and myself.

We spoke briefly after the meeting was over and agreed to talk together at my home. Pierre, aware that I had been slated to be the fourth member of the Marchand team, offered to withdraw from the Mount Royal race and run in Saint-Jean-sur-Richelieu, the only other riding still open. The organizers turned him down cold. Saint-Jean had been represented for some time by the charismatic populist Yvon Dupuis, who had been turfed out of the Liberal Party and was running as an independent. The Liberal organizers were very much afraid that he would win. (In the end, the Liberal candidate defeated him.)

The organizers, fearful that the English-speaking community would reject Trudeau, and that the Jewish community would resent having no Montreal representative in the House of Commons the next time around and would therefore vote for me, put pressure on me to withdraw. I refused, saying that their boast of being a democratic party would be hollow if I did. They backed off.

I had meanwhile discovered, however, that I was playing with a deck stacked against me. The voting delegates had all been chosen before I was allowed to enter the race. In a riding that was 85 per cent anglophone and 15 per cent francophone, the delegates were 50-50. When I finally was allowed to have the list and began calling to ask for support, person after person – among the francophones – was essentially uninformed and said candidly that a certain gentleman had called and told them he was putting their names on a list and would pay the $2 fee required. Knowing none of the candidates, they voted for the one with the French name.

The day before the convention Stuart Smith withdrew. The speeches were well received, the votes were cast, and Pierre won by 152 to my 56. Instinctively, I proposed that his nomination be considered unanimous. I went to the house in the Town of Mount Royal where my supporters were gathered and thanked them for all they had done. Then, still going on instinct, I stopped by at the Trudeau reception in the home of John Ewasew (later a senator) and was very warmly greeted.

Meanwhile something special had happened. As I came down off the stage at the Mount Royal Town Hall, a knot of people were waiting for me, led by Mary Goodman, who subsequently became my best organizer and a cherished friend. They said to me, "The things you stressed in your speech, health and education, are provincial responsibilities. The provincial electoral map has also been redrawn, and we will be in a new riding, D'Arcy McGee. Will you be our candidate?" I told them of my commitment to Jean Marchand and said that I would have to ask him to release me. After a short time he did. Fortunately, D'Arcy McGee was still waiting, and I said yes.

NOMINATION

The Liberal nomination in D'Arcy McGee was an object of interest for a considerable number of people. A young lawyer, Harold Dermer, had already signed up a fair number of party members, and several other people appeared to be testing the waters. Because it was a new riding, it had not yet created its administrative structures, and party authorities had not yet made their presence and their interest felt.

Eric Kierans, the Minister of Health, represented the adjacent riding of Notre-Dame-de-Grâce and had overall responsibility for the English-speaking community. He became aware of my interest and asked to see me. At the end of our conversation, he gave me his blessing and outlined a strategy. At his suggestion, I met with Dermer, who agreed to withdraw and became a supporter. Gradually, a team came together and the work began. Other candidates entered the race and set about signing up voting members. The forms came in by the hundreds, and when the convention took place in the Duke of York's Hussars' Armory on Côte-des-Neiges Road, there were over a thousand voting delegates.

The campaign had turned nasty, with anonymous negative ads and unpleasant smear tactics. They included the ancient trick of mailing out an attack ad that was delivered the day before the convention so that a response was impossible. I attacked no one, although in my convention speech I did decry the anonymous negative campaign. My principal opponent was a lawyer named Louis Orenstein, whom I had never met but with whom I would work cordially in later years when he was president of Mount Sinai Hospital. His supporters had become the officers of the new D'Arcy McGee Liberal Association when it was formed, which made my task all the more difficult. In the end I won a first-ballot victory.

I set out to heal the divisions. The association president, David Kirshenblatt, was cordial, and I prevailed on David Weinstein, an accountant who had been Orenstein's financial manager, to become my official agent. We worked harmoniously together and sailed through the 1966 election campaign to a very large majority. I joined the Liberal caucus and prepared to take my seat in the National Assembly.

# Vignettes

## JEAN LESAGE

Jean Lesage was already a towering figure when I first met him in the spring of 1966. The six years of the Quiet Revolution had brought Quebec dramatically and irreversibly forward into the twentieth century, and he had been the visionary who had traced the path and led the way. It had been prepared by seminal thinkers, who had begun to see light at the end of the long Duplessis tunnel. Georges-Émile Lapalme had been Lesage's predecessor as leader of the Quebec Liberal Party, a brilliant social planner but not a charismatic orator. Father Georges-Henri Lévesque was an influential and provocative teacher at Université Laval, but priests did not often go into politics. It was said that Paul Sauvé, Maurice Duplessis's dauphin, who was felled by a heart attack after less than four months in office, could have been a Quiet Revolutionary. It was Lesage who passed into history.

Before 1960, few would have predicted it. Jean Lesage had been a minister in Lester B. Pearson's federal government, perceived as competent but not as a shining star. A federal career was not necessarily a promising preparation for provincial leadership, and although Antonio Barrette, who succeeded Paul Sauvé, was a less formidable opponent, the 1960 election was no sure thing and was in fact decided by a relatively narrow margin.

Lesage had sensed that a majority was out of reach unless
he appealed to what came to be called Quebec nationalism.
His later slogan, "Maîtres chez nous," contributed to an
impression that he was ambivalent about Canadian unity. He
was not. He was a great admirer of Prime Minister Pearson
and found it difficult to do what he had to do: oppose him
on certain federal-provincial issues. (He had less difficulty
doing so with John Diefenbaker.) He stood his ground, however, when, for example, he disagreed with the way in which
the Canada Pension Plan was structured and insisted on
a Quebec Pension Plan, which he was convinced would be
more secure.

He was not afraid to surround himself with strong personali-
ties: Paul Gérin-Lajoie, whom he had defeated for the leadership and who became Quebec's first Minister of Education;
Georges-Émile Lapalme; and, of course, René Lévesque. He
was always the captain of the ship with a firm hand on the helm.
He was also the team's most effective spokesman, the most
articulate and persuasive advocate of the Quiet Revolution.

In the process, however, he became perceived as arrogant.
When he called the election in 1966, people all over the
province wanted him to be chastened – "taught a lesson" –
with a reduced majority but not defeated. However, so many
people voted in that strategic way that he was, to general surprise, turned out of office. It was a bitter experience, but he
rose to the challenge of being Leader of the Opposition. For
three years he guided and rebuilt the party and prepared his
succession. One August day in 1969 he announced that he
was stepping down.

The three years had not been easy, and caucus support had
not been unanimous. Before his public statement, he gathered those whom he perceived as his loyalists at his summer
home in Lac Beauport, north of Quebec City. I was one of
them. He was dignified and unemotional, and confident –
correctly, as it turned out – about the future of the party.

One of Jean Lesage's outstanding attributes was his encyclo-
pedic knowledge of Quebec's legislation. Reading each section

(article) of a new bill, he would often say, "You can't do that because of section X of Bill Y of 19zz." His sure grasp of precedents and of the overarching philosophy of Quebec legislation was impressive and unique. As a result, when Robert Bourassa became premier, he asked Lesage to be, without fanfare, his government's chief legislative adviser. It was thus that when I brought forward the Environment Quality Act. I had spent several months working with Lesage on every word, struggling with occasional disagreements, and learning at the feet of the master.

My last memory of Jean Lesage is the most extraordinary of all. The 1980 referendum on Quebec sovereignty was a few days away, and a major federalist rally was planned for Quebec City. Lesage was coming out of retirement to be one of the speakers. Three days before the event, he was informed that he had cancer of the larynx. His physicians, including his brother-in-law, who was an ear, nose, and throat specialist, told him that the chances of success of an operation depended on his not using his voice. He responded, "My country is too important to me." And he made the speech.

## ROBERT BOURASSA

Robert Bourassa and I hit it off from the very beginning. We were part of a fairly large group of first-time MNAs who arrived in 1966 – not large enough, however, to bring Jean Lesage back to power – and as we got to know each other, four of us gravitated together: Jean-Paul Lefebvre, Jérôme Choquette, Robert, and myself. We had similar or complementary interests and a common intellectual level, and we began to get together every month or so to discuss issues and think about policies. Lefebvre was our convenor. The first subject we took up was education, and he logically invited Paul Gérin-Lajoie to speak with us. Gérin-Lajoie had been Quebec's first Minister of Education and had given intellectual leadership to the modernization and democratization of the system. He was sensible and pragmatic, and he was generous with his time and his reflections.

After a while, however, a feeling began to grow that Lefebvre's objective was to promote Gérin-Lajoie as a candidate for the leadership of the party, assuming that Jean Lesage would step down after his unexpected defeat. They had run against each other in 1960, and although they had worked together effectively in the cabinet, it was taken for granted that Gérin-Lajoie had not abandoned his ambitions. (Ultimately, he resigned his seat before the leadership convention.)

The meetings of the quadrumvirate petered out, but I continued to see Robert fairly often. We both had the habit of working late into the evening. Our offices were on the same floor. Robert's was much closer to the elevator, and if his light was on, I would stop in. Often he had an interesting visitor, someone knowledgeable in a particular field, and I was able to share in his learning process as he prepared, discreetly, to seek the leadership.

When Jean Lesage did step aside, three hats were thrown into the ring: Claude Wagner's, Pierre Laporte's, and Robert Bourassa's. I was on good terms with all three. Wagner had a law-and-order philosophy with which I did not feel in tune. Laporte, however, had gone out of his way to welcome the class of 1966 and had continued to be a sharp-minded mentor, and I felt a certain degree of obligation towards him. (More members of the caucus supported him than either of the other two candidates.) Robert had come to impress me enormously, and the rumour was circulating that Lesage perceived him as his successor. I wrestled with my decision and came down in favour of Robert.

I went to see Lesage; I thought it appropriate to inform him of my decision. He did not give me a chance to do so. He said that he had wanted to see me because he was concerned about the divisiveness within the party inherent in a leadership contest, and he wanted to have a cadre of people who would remain neutral and incarnate party unity. I asked him how many such people he had recruited, and he said, "Doctor, you're the first." I asked him to ensure that Robert was made aware of his request. In the end, Gérard D.-Levesque and Bernard Pinard remained neutral, but Gérard played a minimal role and Bernard none. I was left alone to preside over the voting.

When Robert emerged victorious and won the 1970 election (in which I vigorously participated), I worried that he might be resentful that I had not given him my expected support. I was also inevitably conscious of the fact that no Jewish M N A had ever been named to the Quebec cabinet. Two days before he announced his team, Robert called me in and appointed me Minister of State attached to Education and to Health. It was obviously less than I had hoped for, and I was inclined to think that if I had joined Robert's team in the leadership contest, I would have had something more substantial. On the other hand, I was not sure that I was fully ready for the challenge of heading a major ministry. In retrospect, things turned out, somewhat later, for the best.

I made some early errors but learned from them and gained Robert's confidence. The old comradeship revived. I became more and more impressed with his leadership. Robert had a particular way of chairing cabinet meetings. He would briefly introduce a subject and invite discussion. Intervening very little, he would let the arguments flow back and forth, often for a considerable time. When there was ultimately quiet, he would define what he perceived to be the consensus – or sometimes his own conclusion – and he would do it so skilfully that everyone would nod in agreement.

It became the conventional wisdom in the cabinet and the caucus that Robert's political instincts were better than anyone else's, and that if we sometimes disagreed with them, he would be proven right and the rest of us wrong. The one dramatic exception was the 1976 election, which he called a year or more before he had to and which changed Quebec history. He misread public opinion, miscalculated the negative impact of his language legislation in both the English-speaking and French-speaking communities, and underestimated the appeal of René Lévesque. There was labour unrest in the province – we were told that it was too dangerous for us to go into the Saguenay–Lac-Saint-Jean ridings – and our campaign played poorly in the media and on the ground. The election of the Parti Québécois was a shock, especially in the English-speaking community. Robert then engendered resentment by vanishing six weeks after the election, headed for Europe to study the European Economic Community.

Some years later he was forgiven and re-elected premier of Quebec. He ended up, on balance, highly regarded, and was one of the longest-serving premiers in the province's history. He was negatively portrayed during and after the October Crisis of 1970. He was said to have been weak and indecisive, unsure of what to do; Pierre Elliott Trudeau was considered to have been in control of the situation. The Bourassa that I knew during those tense weeks was cool and clear-headed and very much in command. He was an extraordinarily courageous leader, unflappable and less egotistical than most, and he deserves to be remembered as such.

Robert Bourassa was a person of vision. The James Bay Project was, on balance, a major achievement, a response to the long-term electricity needs of Quebec and, indeed, of its neighbours. As an economist by profession, he held to the principle that a society must create wealth before it can distribute it. He coined the phrase "profitable federalism," which caused some people to question the depth of his commitment to Canada. When the chips were down, however, he stood clearly for the unity of the country. His public persona was dry and serious; in private he was a warm and humorous person. There were times when he frustrated me, but on balance he earned my profound and genuine loyalty and esteem.


## RENÉ LÉVESQUE

I met René Lévesque for the first time in the fall of 1963. He was Minister of Natural Resources in the Liberal cabinet of

Premier Jean Lesage, and he was clearly the most socially conscious and progressive person in that diverse coalition. After he had piloted the nationalization of electricity through the legislature, he was made Minister of Social Welfare, working in harmonious tandem with Eric Kierans, who had become Minister of Health.

The College of Physicians and Surgeons, of which I was third vice-president, had received an invitation from Lévesque's riding association to provide a speaker about the health insurance program, which was very much in the works, and I was the person chosen. I was told that Lévesque was usually not present at these meetings, except for a brief token appearance towards the end of the evening.

The College having taken a rather positive approach towards medicare, as we came to call it, I was understandably nervous but not unduly apprehensive. I was five or six minutes into my presentation, when the door opened and René Lévesque walked in. He sat at the back, but when my talk was over, it was he who started asking the questions. I am sure that he expected to encounter a reactionary anti-medicare physician. The fact that he did not became the foundation of a mutually respectful and constructive relationship.

When I was elected to the Quebec legislature in 1966, we became colleagues. Since we were on the opposition side of the house, Lévesque became social welfare critic and Kierans took on that role in health. As a physician interested in the management of health care, and as a socially conscious person married to a professor of social work, I became for each of them a leading member of the supporting cast. We generally saw eye to eye on issues, and my relationship with Lévesque was cordial and harmonious.

Then November 1967 came along. The party held a convention, and René Lévesque brought forward a position paper that was essentially a sovereignist manifesto. Paul Gérin-Lajoie presented a competing document, and when the delegates made that their choice, Lévesque resigned. In the turmoil that followed, the media interviewed dozens of people.

Late in the evening I was asked to go down to the television centre in the basement. As I waited my turn, the journalists were taking stock of who remained to be interviewed. They reeled off names: Monsieur Kierans, Monsieur Cliche, Docteur Goldbloom, Monsieur Courcy – and René. Although a political figure, he was still one of them.

The Lévesque departure left a gap: a new social affairs critic had to be named, and it was suggested that I might be it. Émilien Lafrance, an older and rather conservative gentleman for whom I had a warm regard, had been minister before Lévesque, and I went to see him to suggest that the position was rightfully his. He replied that because he had been sidelined in favour of Lévesque, he was unwilling to step in. So I became the critic.

Two months later, Eric Kierans resigned to run for the federal Liberal leadership against Pierre Elliott Trudeau. The post of health critic was now vacant, and I inherited it as well. I dug into my augmented responsibilities and developed a very cordial adversarial relationship with the Union Nationale Minister of Health and Social Welfare, Jean-Paul Cloutier. This continued until the spring of 1970. Then an election was called, and we became the government.

Jean Lesage had resigned as leader of the Quebec Liberal Party, and Robert Bourassa had taken his place. Bourassa asked me to join his cabinet and assigned me the imprecise role of Minister of State Attached to Education and to Health. Claude Castonguay was Minister of Health, and we had a good relationship, but he found no role for me in his department. Guy Saint-Pierre, an engineer, was a surprise appointment as Minister of Education, and he immediately made me a member of his team.

René Lévesque had returned to journalism, and he commented extensively on the new Bourassa government. When he came to Education, he invoked Guy Saint-Pierre's lack of specific experience in that field and suggested that he was not really the minister. He wrote, "I detect behind the throne the fine Florentine hand of the M N A for D'Arcy McGee." I smiled, but I was put out by that twisting of the reality. Guy went on to be an outstanding Minister of Education.

When Lévesque became premier in November 1976, the old friendship and mutual respect revived, but the relationship was necessarily different. Our social consciences continued to bind us together, but our political differences, notably with regard to the unity of Canada, imposed a certain distance.

One recollection of René Lévesque is quite unforgettable. In July 1967 French president Charles de Gaulle came to Montreal for an official visit to Expo. The MNAs were invited, along with other dignitaries, to wait for the general's arrival on the large back balcony of Montreal City Hall. We saw the motorcade pull into the parking lot below, but de Gaulle did not materialize. He went to the small balcony in the front of the building and addressed the crowd, many of whom were carrying "Québec libre!" signs. His brief but historic speech was clearly audible over the loudspeakers. The impact of his closing words was dramatic. Lévesque was in the row in front of Sheila and myself. I happened to be looking back into the stunned faces of the diplomatic corps. Lévesque asked Sheila, "What does Victor think?" She said that I was very disturbed at an inappropriate incursion into our internal affairs, and she asked him, "What do *you* think, Mr Lévesque?" He replied, "I don't know. I haven't made up my mind."

Thinking back, I recall that Prime Minister Lester Pearson, of course upset by "Vive le Québec libre," was even more so by de Gaulle's comparison of his trip up the Chemin du Roy (along the north shore of the St Lawrence River from Quebec to Montreal) to his liberation of Paris in 1944. Mike Pearson said, "This is a free country and there is nothing to liberate here." I recall also that René Lévesque had been a war correspondent, had seen a liberated concentration camp, and had principles; so I understand his ambivalence better today than I did on the spur of the moment.

Many years later, in November of 2012, I attended an event marking the twenty-fifth anniversary of René Lévesque's death. Former premiers Jacques Parizeau, Lucien Bouchard, and

Bernard Landry were there, and when I went over at the end
to shake hands with Landry, he commented that I was the
only federalist present. I said that before Lévesque had
founded the Parti Québécois, he had been a Liberal and I was
his colleague, and we had worked together with a lot of
reciprocal positive feeling. He left a major mark on Quebec
history, and on me.


## PIERRE ELLIOTT TRUDEAU

Pierre and I met in the fall of 1965. We were slated to be team-
mates. We became reluctant opponents. We would remain lifelong friends.

Jean Marchand had asked both of us to join with him and
Gérard Pelletier to run for the House of Commons. The
Liberal Party organization had a seat for Jean and found one
with a bit of difficulty for Gérard, but then ran into a problem.
Pierre was not widely known and was regarded as something of
a dilettante. His membership in Marchand's team had been
announced; mine had not. Over Jean's objections, we were
told to run in the same riding, Mount Royal. We met several
times to talk the situation through. We were both political neo-
phytes, and the organizers paid us no heed. Pierre won and
went on to make history. There was no enmity between us.

One evening prior to the Mount Royal convention, Pierre
and I were to meet at my house. Sheila and I had been invited
to a wedding, the first time that two of my former patients
were getting married. Our fifteen-year-old daughter, Susan,
was at home. The wedding ceremony and reception were
greatly delayed, and I called Susan to say that a Mr Trudeau
would be coming to see me and would undoubtedly arrive
before we got home. She asked if she should speak with him
in French or in English. I suggested that she greet him in
French, and that he would then switch to English. He did not,
and she spent forty-five valiant minutes in her second language. Pierre never forgot.

Michael, in his pyjamas, was hiding under the dining-room table and heard the whole conversation. He recalls that Pierre asked Susan to play the piano and complimented her on her performance. Three years later Pierre became prime minister of Canada, and we were invited to the reception following his swearing-in. Sheila was unable to go, and I asked Susan to accompany me. We patiently edged our way along until we were standing behind Pierre. He turned and saw us and said, "Susan, you've changed your hair!" And he inquired about her piano playing.

I became a Quebec M N A and subsequently a minister. My riding overlapped much of Pierre's federal one, so we would meet at local events. As a minister, I participated in a number of federal-provincial conferences, and he was often present. The mutual cordiality was unfailing. But inevitably, we some-times saw things differently. Pierre's multiculturalism policy did not sit well with Quebec – it does not to this day – where preoccupation with the preservation of a language and a cul-ture predominates over the diversification of society and issues of accommodation. I was greatly troubled by the resent-ment engendered in western Canada by Pierre's National Energy Policy and by the resultant political cleavage in the country. And although I shared Pierre's commitment to the unity of Canada, I wished that he would reach out more cor-dially to the nationalists in Quebec society. It was a recurring paradox that Pierre would sweep Quebec – and so would René Lévesque. It was certainly a "favourite son" phenom-enon, but it was also a reflection of Quebecers' attachment to the different facets of their identity.

Ours was not a close friendship, but it was a real one. I once had dinner with him, just the two of us, at 24 Sussex Drive. He asked me to look at one of the boys, who had a small problem. He spoke with me discreetly about Margaret and about father-hood. Despite his massive and demanding responsibilities as prime minister, he was an exemplary parent.

In the 1990s, when I was Commissioner of Official Lan-guages of Canada, I was invited to speak at an event organized by *Cité Libre*, the provocative publication of high intellectual quality in which Pierre had been actively involved before his entry into public life. He was in the audience, and I was very much aware that it had been he who in 1969 had brought in the Official Languages Act, which created the position of commissioner. He came up to speak to me afterwards and said, "Well, they chose the right person." I did not see him again. I attended his funeral in Notre Dame Basilica. He was the most remarkable and most brilliant Canadian I was ever privileged to know.

# Minister, 1970–1976

## THE ENVIRONMENT

In the summer of 1970 I wrote to Premier Robert Bourassa to put forward my concern that there were two areas in which, as a government, we were not carrying our weight. One was my pediatrician's perception that we were not doing enough for children: protecting them from the effects of poverty, improving measures against various diseases, preventing accidents. The other was a coherent plan for the protection of the environment. Robert did not immediately respond. One day in September, as I passed him in a corridor, he said something cryptic about things moving in a positive direction. In mid-December he announced my appointment as Quebec's first Minister of the Environment.

Because he had criticized the previous government for having too many ministries, Bourassa chose not to make Environment an autonomous department. A contest immediately arose between Natural Resources and Municipal Affairs. I leaned towards Natural Resources, and I had a good relationship with the minister, Gilles Massé. The Minister of Municipal Affairs, Maurice Tessier, whom at that time I did not know as well, was, however, more persuasive. He argued that the major environmental problems were treating sewage and providing clean water, which were municipal responsibilities, and that there were already teams in his ministry responsible for those areas. He won out. Claude Castonguay, the Minister of Health, became conspicuously helpful. He had a team responsible for air quality and a sector entitled Public Health, and he spontaneously transferred them to the new entity.

I was assigned a deputy minister, Dr J.-Benoît Bundock. Dr Bundock was an old hand, a common-sense pragmatist, and together we set out to shape a ministry. It seemed to me inefficient that an industry or a municipality be visited separately by an air team and a water team, and so I established an industry sector and a municipal sector. A small team was responsible for lake water quality, a major problem throughout Quebec because of untreated sewage from lakeside cottages and sometimes from municipalities; it was led by a fearlessly critical and undisciplined individual named Tony LeSauteur, and I learned to appreciate his commitment and to give him support. (He expressed his appreciation in an autobiography that he wrote many years later.)

There was also an autonomous body, the Régie des Eaux du Québec, and it made sense to absorb it into the Ministry of the Environment. One of its five members stood out for his knowledge, his judgment, and his vision. When it came time, two years later, to move forward into a new phase with the adoption of Quebec's first Environment Quality Act, Dr Bundock was approaching retirement, and I chose Gilles Jolicoeur to be the new deputy minister. (The other members of the Régie were appointed to the Quebec Municipal Commission.)

Writing the Environment Quality Act was a major undertaking. Premier Bourassa asked former premier Jean Lesage to take on this responsibility, and I had the privilege and the pleasure of working with him for over a year – and learning enormously in the process. We had a number of discussions over words, phrases, and concepts. Lesage generally prevailed, but I did win one epic argument. I proposed a section on waste management, and Lesage said, "You don't *manage* waste, you *dispose of* it." Eventually I persuaded him that recycling and composting were very different from dumping garbage in a landfill.

With the coming into force of the act, we set out to meet with industries and municipalities, and to encourage awareness and support in public opinion. When, in 1973, I became Minister of Municipal Affairs as well, I was able to fund municipal sewage-treatment and water-supply systems and to identify a (too small) number of lakes each year for cleanup. We obtained improvement in major industries: pulp and paper, oil refineries, aluminum smelting. I travelled all over the province to meet with municipal officials and community organizations. We knew that we were making small dents in a massive problem, but we had begun.

One of the most conspicuous problems in Quebec was the Union Carbide plant in Beauharnois. Often, when I was flying back and forth between Montreal and Quebec City, the plane would swing out over that area, and I would have a clear view of the broad plume of smoke from the plant's chimneys being carried by the prevailing winds directly over Montreal and blanketing the island. Union Carbide had a vice-president named Alex Hainey, who became my interlocutor and worked tirelessly to devise a de-pollution system. His only request, which was absolutely fair, was that any competitor be required to de-pollute at the same time. It was a major undertaking, and it took a couple of years, but it was ultimately gratifying to see the plume of smoke diminished to something of a wisp.

I learned that, from the air, one had a clear view of pollution flowing into lakes and streams, and that this was generally not perceptible at ground level. The titanium plants on the south shore of the St Lawrence east of Montreal were a conspicuous example, and one that proved much more difficult to correct. We had a fair amount of knowledge when we began, but we learned more and more as we went along, and we became more effective in working with industries to diminish their environmental impact.

Public opinion was not against us, but it was not supportive either. There were two pressure groups, one French-speaking and the other English-speaking, which were vocal and critical, but the public in general gave the environment no thought and needed to be educated. Most people took for granted that pollutants in the air would simply dissipate, and that the absorptive capacities of lakes, rivers, and especially oceans were unlimited. A communications strategy was an immediate necessity.

The notion that unlimited economic growth and industrial development were unquestionable values was an enormous challenge to overcome. The idea of sustainability was absent from our vocabulary and from our thoughts, and the systematic evaluation of the environmental impacts of a project or an industry was unheard of. We were not quite starting from scratch, but we had a steep mountain to climb. There was even a spiritual, religious aspect to our task. The story of Creation in the Book of Genesis gives human beings stewardship over the earth and over its flora and fauna, and we cannot shrug off that responsibility. Clergy became important allies. We also had to inculcate in the public the notion of generational obligation – that we might get away with polluting our environment and suffer minimal inconvenience and harm, but that it was irresponsible to oblige our children and our grandchildren to inherit an environment that would endanger their health and their children's development.

In April 1971 Premier Bourassa announced his epic James Bay Project. He did not anticipate that the first member of his team to be on the firing line from public opinion would be his Minister of the Environment. Ecological impacts were the earliest concerns to come forward, and I was called upon repeatedly to face the media, to address groups such as the Canadian Zoological Society (where I met, at McGill University, with a substantial group of young Aboriginal Quebecers), and to devise an action program.

We had a small budget and could not undertake a real program of environmental assessment and protection. What we were able to do, however, at Gilles Jolicoeur's suggestion, was to produce a compilation of the studies needed, which were subsequently implemented in significant measure by Hydro-Québec. Indeed, some years later a major exhibition, called *Les Floralies*, was presented in the Old Port of Montreal. I came upon a shed in which Hydro-Québec's James Bay Development Corporation exhibited a plant that it had discovered and developed, which took root in the minimal topsoil of the James Bay area and prevented erosion.

In 1972 the United Nations decided to convene a conference on the environment. It was held in Stockholm, Sweden. The Canadian delegation was headed by the federal minister, Jack Davis, and two provincial ministers were invited to join the team. I was one of them. Maurice Strong of Canada was the principal moving spirit behind the conference, and he was extremely helpful to the Canadian delegation. Considering that this was an unprecedented and innovative undertaking, it was rather well organized. Each of us had the honour of occupying Canada's chair from time to time in the plenary sessions, and each of us was assigned to a working group as well. I drew the one on social issues and was able to sponsor a resolution on the improvement of access infrastructure for handicapped persons.

The full delegation met for an hour each morning to discuss issues and determine positions. It was not possible, of course, to anticipate everything that might be brought forward, and although one or more staff persons were with us in each working group, we sometimes had to make an on-the-spot determination of what Canada's position should be. I voted in support of a resolution regarding consideration for low-income people, and was subsequently chewed out by two surly American delegates for having been too far to the left.

There were two fundamental conclusions from the conference. One was that we should come together again in four years' time. The other was to create a United Nations Centre for the Environment. Three or four countries, including

Canada, competed for it, and Kenya was chosen. Geoffrey Bruce, the general secretary of the Canadian delegation, subsequently went to Nairobi to become its head.

Four years later a second UN conference was organized, this time in Vancouver. Again, I was invited to be one of Canada's official delegates – indeed, a vice-chairperson of the team. This was the first UN conference in which Communist China participated, and its half-dozen representatives were low-key in their behaviour but visually conspicuous in their pale blue Mao Zedong suits. One morning I was occupying Canada's seat in the plenary, and one of our staff came over to say that a Chinese delegate had approached him with a request in a language he could not understand; maybe I, whom he perceived as more of a linguist, could manage to effect communication. He brought the gentleman over, and he turned out to be speaking stilted but elegant French. He was asking to meet our federal minister, which was readily arranged.

There was widespread excitement in Vancouver because the ambassador assigned to the American delegation was Shirley Temple Black, the child star of the movies of my youth. At a reception early on, I was introduced to her. She was cold, curt, and dismissive. My admiring memories evaporated.

At both conferences the quality of our delegation was impressive. In Stockholm we were six official delegates and close to forty senior civil servants. In Vancouver, as the host country, we had nine delegates and fifty staff. Several of the public servants were world-class professionals in their fields and made leading-edge contributions in the working groups to which they were assigned.

The federal minister in Vancouver was my good friend Barney Danson of Toronto. Because we were the host country, he was designated at the opening session to be overall chairman of the conference, and his colleague Ron Basford of Vancouver took over as head of our delegation. A key public servant was H. Peter Oberlander, a comrade from my McGill days who had graduated in architecture in the convocation at which I had graduated in medicine. Peter's wife, Cornelia Hahn, was, and is, Canada's outstanding landscape architect. Peter was Deputy Minister of Housing, and the conference was titled Human Settlements. It is a United Nations tradition that at the close of a conference, the massive documentation produced is bequeathed to the host country and, indeed, to the host city. The beneficiary was the University of British Columbia, which created a Centre on Human Settlements, and Peter left the federal public service to become its director. It was an opportunity to be seized, and it made Canada a world leader in the field.

As time went by, there was less and less resistance to environmental protection standards and measures. We had launched an irreversible process, but its inevitability was not widely recognized back in 1970. Robert Bourassa deserves significant credit for having said yes.

There was an additional occasion on which he surprised me by saying yes. I had been made aware, primarily by Tony LeSauteur, that the Boucherville Islands had been put up for sale and were on the verge of being bought by a developer. Bunched together just downstream from downtown Montreal – the Lafontaine Tunnel emerges from under the St Lawrence and crosses their western extremity – they were home to nesting birds, to fish spawning in their shallows, and to some small-scale farming. Their natural state deserved to be saved. The price tag was a million dollars, which my ministry did not have, and I put together a proposal that I brought to cabinet. I anticipated a good deal of resistance, but there was absolutely none, and Robert announced the purchase to unequivocal approval.

When people ask me to reflect on what may have been my most significant achievement in public life, they rather expect me to cite the successful completion of the Olympic installations in 1976, but for me it was being the pioneer of environmental protection in Quebec.

## THE OCTOBER CRISIS

A great, great deal has been written and said about the October Crisis of 1970. Hindsight has generated sure-handed wisdom about what should have been done or not done. Living it from the inside was a different story. We now know how few people were involved. That fact was by no means evident at the time. The risk of underestimating the enemy was a constant preoccupation. The RCMP, the Sûreté du Québec, and the Montreal Urban Community Police worked closely together and provided the cabinet with daily briefings, but they were obliged to offer more conjecture than information.

Premier Robert Bourassa decided that the cabinet should be in Montreal rather than Quebec City. That was widely interpreted as evidence of weakness, of panic, and of incompetence. In fact, it was because the nerve centre of police operations was in Montreal, and up-to-the-minute briefings and strategic decision-making were possible at short notice, two or three times a day if necessary.

Robert was portrayed as weak and vacillating, overwhelmed by events and dependent on the sure hand (and vigorous rhetoric) of Pierre Elliott Trudeau. It was stated, and believed, that Trudeau chose and imposed the War Measures Act. People such as Claude Ryan and René Lévesque, with a dozen or so others, affirmed that the situation was out of control and that an emergency unity government, consisting primarily of themselves, should come into being – by an unspecified mechanism – and take over.

What impressed me throughout the crisis was the premier's calmness and clear judgment. He and his wife, Andrée, were very much present on that upper floor of the Queen Elizabeth Hotel where the cabinet was quartered – a half-dozen blocks from the premier's office in the Hydro-Québec building where our formal meetings took place – and both of them made sure that each of us took advantage of opportunities to rest and that we felt confident that a firm hand was on the tiller.

The police forces, in their daily reports, painted a picture of a widespread and deep-rooted insurrection – which, of course, was part of the communications strategy of the Front de libération du Québec (FLQ). They affirmed that they had a list of subversive individuals, many of whom could be presumed to be masterminding the FLQ operations, and they urged that these persons be preventively rounded up and intensively interrogated. They put the figure at 1,100 people.

The more emotional among us, including Justice Minister Jérôme Choquette, gave credence to the police recommendation. Robert remained unconvinced for a number of days, but finally accepted the argument, in the face of the lack of progress. The list was reduced to some 600, the roundup was carried out – and nothing was achieved. No charges were ever brought against any of these individuals, and no pertinent information was communicated to us. The discussions concerning the War Measures Act were also stressful and divisive. Again, the premier was cool and questioning, and took time to be convinced. Finally, he agreed, and a special messenger was sent to Ottawa, carrying the formal request that the WMA be invoked.

On a personal level, the stress and the uncertainty were enormous. A cabinet minister could not walk away or even be absent. Susan and Michael were at university in Boston; Jonathan was at school in Montreal. We decided that, in the face of the unknown danger, it was preferable that Sheila and Jonathan leave. Shepherded by the RCMP, they flew to Toronto, where they were briefly sheltered by our friends Renee and Ivor Simmons, and then went on to New York – although they were forbidden by the RCMP to stay with Sheila's parents – and to Boston. Jonathan had applied to Milton Academy, south of the city, for the following year. I called the school, explained the circumstances, and asked if he could be admitted forthwith. The administrators kindly squeezed him in.

Soldiers mounted guard around our house, which did not thrill the neighbours. Rather than use our own cars, we were driven everywhere, including back and forth to Quebec City, in Quebec provincial police vehicles, which kept in constant radio contact with headquarters. The Sûreté posted officers all night in the Manoir d'Auteuil, the converted house on the street of the same name where I had a regular room. At the proprietor's request, I moved out and was welcomed in the Hotel Victoria, where Robert Bourassa had taken over a well-guarded floor and had a vacant room. When I left my National Assembly or ministry office in the late evening, I would often ask the Sûreté officer to stop by the local command headquarters on Saint-Cyrille (now René-Lévesque) Boulevard, where a lieutenant with whom I had struck up an acquaintance would brief me on the search operations and on the ongoing analysis of the FLQ threat.

The FLQ issued communiqués and sent messages and ultimatums, often through a lawyer, Robert Lemieux, who acted as intermediary. (Robert Bourassa had named a representative, Robert Demers, to relate one-on-one with this gentleman.) Each time, cabinet met to consider how to respond. We were deeply conscious of our responsibility for the life of Pierre Laporte, our cabinet colleague, who had been kidnapped in broad daylight, and for that of James Richard Cross, the British consul general, who had been taken at gunpoint from his home, and it was with real anguish that we repeatedly concluded that we could not give in to blackmail. To do so would undoubtedly encourage more blackmail from the FLQ and from imitators, destroy the authority of government, and destabilize civil society.

I was offered a couple of days off, and Sheila, who had returned home, and I went to Boston to see the children. (It was recommended by the RCMP that ministers travel under an assumed name, and I chose Jack Daniels.) While we were there, a call came in from Paul Desrochers, Robert Bourassa's right-hand man, informing me that Pierre Laporte's body had been found in the trunk of a car. Pierre had been a good friend – not a close one but a fountain of political knowledge and strategic sense. It was a shocking loss. I headed back for the funeral, held under heavy guard – strictly controlled access, snipers with binoculars on the roofs of Notre Dame Basilica and adjacent buildings, helicopters overhead – and plunged back into the stress of the uncertainty.

The denouement finally came with the localization of the FLQ's house in which James Cross was being held prisoner. He was released unharmed, and the kidnappers were allowed to fly to Cuba. The tension gradually deflated, cabinet function returned to normal, and the true dimensions of the uprising came into focus. (My colleague William Tetley has provided a helpful diary of the crisis.) The second-guessing began. My admiration for Robert Bourassa, already appreciable, had gone up a large notch.


### THE OLYMPICS

One morning in November 1975 a call came in shortly after nine, summoning me to a meeting at eleven in the premier's office. The subject was not specified, but it was made clear that attendance was not optional. The room was jammed with more than thirty people, all standing expectantly. There were senior ministers such as Raymond Garneau and Gérard D.-Levesque, deputy ministers such as Claude Rouleau, lawyers specialized in the writing of legislative texts, and senior members of the premier's staff. A few undoubtedly knew what was going to be announced; the majority of us did not.

Robert Bourassa did not keep us waiting long. He voiced the concern, which I and others had been feeling for some time, that the construction of the Olympic facilities was seriously behind schedule and that the reputation of Montreal, of Quebec, and of Canada was at risk, and he told us that he had decided that the province should take over. A bill for that purpose had been prepared, and it would be on the order paper of the National Assembly the following day.

As people started to file out, the premier held me back.
He told me that I would be the legislative sponsor of the bill.
"After all," he said, "we are intervening in the life of our largest municipality, and it is logical that the Minister of Municipal Affairs be the government's spokesperson." When I sat
down and read through the bill, I noticed en passant that
the lieutenant-governor-in-council (nominally the cabinet
but in reality the premier) would be naming a minister to be
responsible for its implementation. I gave that no further
thought. A few days later, however, after I had presented the
bill in first reading and had opened and closed the debate in
second reading, Robert informed me that it would be me.

It was, as in *The Godfather*, an offer I could not refuse. But I
realized that I was at risk of political suicide. Finance Minister
Raymond Garneau, Claude Rouleau's first choice upon his
appointment as president of the Olympic Installations Board,
was not expendable. I was.

The Olympic Installations Board had five members. I was
not one of them. I was, however, the person who had to
respond to questions in the legislature and from the media,
and so I asked to attend all their meetings. I knew only two of
the members: Rouleau, whom I had encountered in his role as
deputy minister, and Gerry Fitzpatrick, an engineer whose five
children I had looked after and who was the only member who
had experience with major construction projects. Gerry repeatedly expressed the opinion that the job could not be done.

At the end of the first OIB meeting, in early January 1976, I
took Rouleau aside and asked him, "What are our chances of
pulling this off?" He answered, "Twenty per cent." Time passed,
progress was made, and the mood brightened. Fitzpatrick,
however, kept saying, "We're not going to make it." We pressed
on. We had no choice.

The Olympic Games are not awarded to a country or a province, but to a city. Montreal mayor Jean Drapeau had a pen-
chant for the grandiose. Expo '67 had been an enormous
success in that regard and had enhanced the city's (and its

mayor's) international status. The federal and provincial governments could not refuse him their support, and in 1970 the International Olympic Committee gave him the prize.

Resisting pressures to choose a Canadian and, if possible, a Quebec architect, the mayor designated the Frenchman Roger Taillibert, whose Parc des Princes stadium in Paris had impressed him. Taillibert had never worked in a winter climate as severe as that of Montreal, and he came forward with complex technology that was unfamiliar to most people. The concrete beams that would support the roof had to be reinforced with steel rods, which had to be held under tension until the concrete hardened. Multiple motors were needed to open and close the retractable canvas-like roof, and their coordination (and their reliability) proved an enormous and ultimately insurmountable challenge. Construction lagged behind schedule, with the result that components which would have been easy to install in summer weather became major problems. Costs escalated. In France the architect remains in charge of the project throughout the construction. In North America he or she does not. This source of tension further complicated the task.

A personal anecdote: As the construction of the stadium neared completion, we were obliged to allow V I P groups to visit it. One such group was led by Andrée Bourassa, the premier's wife. Sheila was included. Suddenly, their path was crossed by two men, one of whom was Roger Taillibert. He recognized Andrée and stopped to talk. Sheila asked him, "Mr. Taillibert, are you not concerned about the escalation of the costs?" Not knowing that he was speaking to the minister's wife, he said, "Madam, when one is building the Cathedral of Chartres, one does not count the cost."

Mayor Drapeau had entrusted the project to the city's Department of Public Works. It had never undertaken anything of this magnitude. (Neither, essentially, had anyone else.) It was Premier Bourassa's conclusion that the department was overwhelmed which brought him to intervene.

Another significant player was COJO, the Organizing Committee of the Olympic Games, headed by Roger Rousseau. He had been Canada's ambassador to Cameroon when I had been there in 1972 to represent Quebec at the opening of Cardinal Paul-Émile Léger's hospital for physically handicapped children. When I became the Minister Responsible for the Olympics, we went to his office in the building next to City Hall and telephoned Lord Killanin, the Irish peer who was president of the International Olympic Committee. The IOC had understandably been increasingly concerned about the progress of the construction, and rumours were rife that the Games would be transferred to a city which had previously held them and had the installations already available. Incredibly, Michael Killanin trusted this new and unknown voice on the other side of the Atlantic. He gave me his unwavering confidence and became a warm and lifelong friend.

The 1976 Winter Games took place at the beginning of February in Innsbruck, Austria. The IOC met the day before the opening ceremonies, and I appeared before the committee to report our progress and straightforwardly answer all its questions. From that point on, the doubts gradually receded. In June I held press conferences in Paris and New York, with Lord Killanin at my side, and coped with such scepticism as remained.

The real hero of the Olympic construction was a man named Roger Trudeau. He was nearing retirement as Quebec's Deputy Minister of Public Works, but he took over the jobsite and brought order out of chaos. He was there at six o'clock every morning and stayed well into the evening. He was calm and clearheaded, and he knew what he was doing.

The city, panicking in the face of the delays, had brought crane after crane into the stadium and added hundreds of men to the workforce. Simply put, they were getting in each other's way. Roger Trudeau reduced the cranes from eighty-four to ten or twelve, cut back the workforce, and simplified the work. He completed one section of the stands and then moved to its neighbour. Steadily, the oval took shape. Roger introduced something which, strangely, had not existed: a daily jobsite meeting of the general contractor, the subcontractors, and the workers' representatives. The agenda was simple: what went wrong today, how can we fix it, and how can we prevent it from happening again?

By Easter it looked as if we were going to succeed. Roger Trudeau proposed that we open the jobsite to the public. The floor of the stadium was still a sea of mud, but he laid boards across it and defined a pathway through the stands. We reserved Good Friday for the workmen and their families and invited the public for Saturday and Sunday. Thousands of people came.

I spent all three days there, greeting people as they came through. I realized that if I went with the flow, I would speak with only the people who were near me, so I went to the exit and walked repeatedly back through the stream of visitors. Notwithstanding my tensions with Jean Drapeau, I felt that the time had come for a gesture of cordiality. I invited him to join me for the Sunday morning, and we spent two hours greeting people together.

Those tensions, however, were not trivial. As construction problems multiplied, delays accumulated, and costs escalated, I had twice, as Minister of Municipal Affairs, convened public hearings before a parliamentary committee. Drapeau put on his characteristic bravura performance, but I had to express the scepticism and concern which were so widely felt – and which then culminated in our takeover. (The mayor, dismissive of concerns about costs, had memorably said that the Olympics could no more have a deficit than a man could have a baby. Shortly after, a cartoon, by Aislin in *The Gazette*, portrayed a pregnant Jean Drapeau on the telephone, saying, "Ello, Morgentaler?" – that is, seeking an abortion.)

The low point came when the mayor decided that there had to be a pedestrian tunnel under Sherbrooke Street for access to the stadium. Dozens of hundred-year-old trees were in the way, and one day he sent out crews at six a.m. to cut them all down, presenting the public – and the Minister of the Environment and of Municipal Affairs – with an ugly *fait accompli* when the day dawned. I was furious and deeply saddened. Drapeau was sarcastic in subsequent interviews, and public opinion reproached his meanness.

Jean Drapeau and I ended up, despite everything, on good terms. I saw him last on 24 June 1991. We met in the receiving line at Premier Bourassa's Saint-Jean-Baptiste Day reception at the Botanical Gardens, across the street from the stadium, and he congratulated me on my appointment as Commissioner of Official Languages. He was an unforgettable character, with a taste for the monumental, and he did some good for Montreal, but on balance, he left a mixed legacy.

In all of this I, of course, had no construction expertise to offer. I do not deserve to be called "the man who saved the Olympics." Apart from fielding all the questions in the National Assembly, I made two contributions. One – it was not my idea, but I latched onto it – was the creation of a six-man task force to spread out over the jobsite and listen to workers' complaints. These were reported promptly and dealt with, so that they did not build into union grievances. The other was that I welcomed the media. Jean Drapeau had kept them off the jobsite and responded to their questions with reassurances rather than details. I convened them on the first Monday of every month, personally conducted a tour of the installations, and then – with Claude Rouleau and Roger Trudeau – spent an hour or more responding fully to their questions.

I faced one particularly sensitive and significant problem. These were the first Summer Games after Munich in 1972, where Israeli athletes had been murdered by terrorists. It went without saying that this time they required special protection. I worked closely with Israeli Consul General Ariel Peter Aran, thinking through their housing arrangements and their movements. I suggested the top floor of the Olympic Village, but Peter vetoed that idea because of the possibility of a helicopter landing on the roof. (We put the athletes five or six floors down.) All went well, but the worries persisted until the Games were over.

We held a religious service in memory of those athletes killed in Munich. It was organized by the Jewish community, not by the international or local Olympic authorities, but it was clearly an official part of our Olympic program. Hundreds of people filled Shaar Hashomayim Synagogue, and Premier Robert Bourassa and Prime Minister Pierre Elliott Trudeau were among the speakers. (I wanted to be there well in advance, and Robert very kindly stopped by to pick up Sheila.) The words and the music were deeply moving, and it is profoundly regrettable that the International Olympic Committee has never been willing to make this commemoration a tradition.

Another personal anecdote: During the Games, as the Minister Responsible I was able to attend any and all events. I concentrated on track and field, that having been my focus in high school. There was a young woman on the Israeli team who was entered in the 100-metre dash. Peter Aran had estimated, accurately, that she would reach the semi-finals but not the final. She came fifth in her semi-final heat, but someone among the first four was disqualified, and there she was in the final. Peter did not have a ticket. I brought him in as my guest. We took seats in the stands, and immediately behind us were Roger Trudeau and Claude Rouleau. I introduced Peter and identified who they were, and he congratulated them on the construction of the facilities. Immediately, both of them replied, "Congratulations for Entebbe!" – the daring rescue by Israeli commandos of hostages kidnapped at an airport in Uganda.

We had completed the construction and turned the installations over to COJO at a modest ceremony on the floor of the stadium. Robert Bourassa, Roger Rousseau, Claude Rouleau, Jean Drapeau, and myself were present. I then bowed out of the picture. On the day of the Opening Ceremonies, 19 July, there was a luncheon for dignitaries under the stands. At the appropriate moment, we were led through into the stadium. I had seen it empty dozens of times, and I was unprepared for the emotional impact of seeing it filled with 73,000 people, and for the sense of being partly responsible for their being there.

## LEAVING POLITICS

When Robert Bourassa resigned the party leadership, six weeks after the defeat of November 1976, interim direction was entrusted to Gérard D.-Levesque. Universally liked and respected – on both sides of the house – he was the obvious choice and did an outstanding job. The ongoing leadership was his for the asking, but he had never in the past wanted to be a candidate for it, and he rejected the pressure that many of us now exerted on him.

Notwithstanding his effectiveness and his willingness to carry on, a mass psychology of anxiety developed over the lack of a permanent leader. A number of caucus members perceived Claude Ryan, publisher of *Le Devoir* and a leading intellectual, as the party's saviour. I knew Claude fairly well and had a good deal of respect for him, but thought him lacking in political instincts and in charismatic personality. When Raymond Garneau threw his hat in the ring, I took on a leading role in his campaign. Raymond had experience in public life and a sense of political strategy; Claude did not, and I did not think he could convert from his intellectual approach to a politically persuasive one. I was right.

We had a campaign song, for which I wrote the words to the tune of "The Battle Hymn of the Republic":

L'avenir, c'est Raymond Garneau!
L'avenir, c'est Raymond Garneau!
L'avenir, c'est Raymond Garneau!
Il faut, il faut Garneau!

Claude Ryan, however, emerged the winner, and he proved to be a thoroughly vindictive one. He convened a meeting of the caucus, and my colleagues who had supported Raymond Garneau asked me to speak on their behalf. I welcomed Claude, spoke of party unity, and assured him of our loyalty and support. He said not one word in response and called for the next item on the agenda. He stripped me of my parliamentary responsibilities – although some months later, at the urging of colleagues, he restored them – and was uncommunicative and cold.

One day I received a note from a friend, Ruth Tannenbaum, enclosing an ad she had clipped from a newspaper. The Canadian Council of Christians and Jews was seeking a chief executive officer. She suggested that the position would be a natural for me. I went to see Claude and told him that I was considering applying for this position. Some weeks later I called on him again, to inform him that I had submitted my candidacy. I saw him a third time to say that I had been short-listed and was going for interviews. On none of these occasions did he say that I was needed in the caucus. The message was clear, and when on a fourth visit I told him I had accepted the position, he simply wished me well.

In the tradition of the Quebec legislature, when one resigns one's seat in the course of a session, one gives a farewell address. I was touched at how full the galleries were: waitresses from the parliamentary restaurant, stenographers who transcribed the proceedings, members of the administrative and support staffs. People on both sides of the house shook my hand. Many have remained friends to this day.

Those thirteen and a half years in public life were filled with intellectual challenge and with a sense of democracy in action. They were mind-expanding, particularly because one had to contribute to debates on subjects outside one's field of expertise. My French was good when I arrived in the National Assembly, but it needed improvement and I worked at polishing it. I acquired a good reputation among the ste-nographers who transcribed the debates.

I had always had the habit, as for example when making house calls, of listening to the car radio in French. One day, a few years after I had left politics, I was tuned in to Jean Cournoyer and Jean Lapierre on C K V L . Their topic was the quality of French spoken in Quebec, and Lapierre remarked to Cournoyer that he must have encountered positives and negatives during his years in the National Assembly.

Cournoyer confirmed that experience and mentioned three or four people whose French he had admired. Then he said, "One person who always seemed to come up with the right word was Victor Goldbloom."

And Jean Lapierre replied, "Yes, but he speaks so slowly that he gives himself the time to come up with the right word …"

My swearing in as a cabinet minister in 1970.

Members of the Bourassa cabinet in 1970: Pierre Laporte, Bernard Pinard, Gérard D. Levesque, Claire Kirkland Casgrain, Claude Castonguay, Jérome Choquette, and Guy St-Pierre.

Me with Prime Minister Pierre Elliott Trudeau around 1970. In 1965 we had run against each other for the federal Liberal nomination in the riding of Mount Royal.

Lac des Becs-Scies, 1971. Quebec is a province of lakes, and those with habitations were almost all polluted, so as Minister of the Environment improving their water quality was a major challenge. Credit: Gerry Davidson, *Montreal Star.*

Jean Chrétien, Cardinal Paul-Émile Léger, and me at the opening of the Cardinal's Centre for handicapped children in Yaoundé, Cameroun, in 1972.

Campaigning with Premier Robert Bourassa during the difficult election of 1976. Credit: Jean-Pierre Rivest, *The Gazette*.

The Olympic Stadium construction site at the time when I was given the responsibility of overseeing the completion of the Olympic installations, October to December 1975.

As Minister Responsible for the Olympic Installations Board, I regularly led media tours of the Olympic Stadium jobsite. This photo was taken in January 1976.

Cartoon by Terry Mosher (Aislin) in *The Gazette* in 1976.

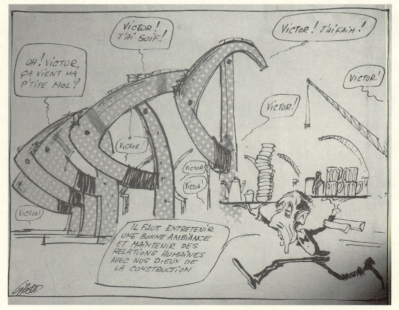

Cartoon by Girerd in Montreal's *La Presse* in 1976.

Jean Drapeau, right, and me at the ceremonial turning over of the Olympic installations to the Comité organisateur des jeux olympiques (COJO) on 13 June 1976.

With Ambassador Roger Rousseau, head of the local organizing group, and Lord Michael Killanin, president of the International Olympic Committee, at the Olympic Velodrome in July 1976. Credit: Canadian Press wire photo.

The Montreal Olympics were the first summer games since the murder of Israeli athletes at the Olympic Games in Munich in 1972. I am speaking here to the Canadian Associates of the Weizmann Institute.

Raymond Garneau and me. I was very proud to support Raymond in his
leadership bid in 1978.

Meeting with Bedouin Sheikh Ibrahim in his home at Beer Sheva, Israel,
in 1973.

I meet with Pope John Paul II at the Vatican on behalf of the International Council of Christians and Jews in 1984.

Sheila and me with the former president of the USSR, Mikhail Gorbachev, in 1992.

Receiving an honorary degree from McGill University in 1992, with Canadian astronaut Roberta Bondar, and Barbara Whitley, a long-time stalwart of Montreal's English-language cultural scene. Credit: McGill University.

Sheila's installation as a member of the Order of Canada by Governor General Roméo LeBlanc in 1998.

Being installed as a companion of the Order of Canada by Governor General Adrienne Clarkson in 2000.

Sheila and me in Israel at the dedication of a forest in my name by the Jewish National Fund of Canada.

Receiving the Papal Order of Saint Sylvester, given by Pope Benedict XVI, from Cardinal Jean-Claude Turcotte in 2012.

Sheila and me in 2013, when the Quebec Community Groups Network recognized us by creating a community service award in our honour.

Portrait of me by Eva Prager.

Me about 1996.

# Dialogue

## CHRISTIAN-JEWISH RELATIONS

My interest in Christian-Jewish relations went back quite a long way. In the late 1950s I had been asked to be part of a dialogue that was initiated by Jesuit fathers who were faculty members at Loyola College, which later merged with Sir George Williams to form Concordia University. It was an intellectually stimulating exercise, calling on all that I had learned about Judaism and obliging me to learn a great deal more.

After two years or so, I said to my Jewish fellow participants that, good as this dialogue was, it was of limited value because we were not in any such communication with the French-speaking majority community. I took action accordingly and made contact with Léon Lortie, a world-renowned professor of chemistry at the Université de Montréal, whom I had encountered in my student days when he came as a guest lecturer to McGill. He and Judge Harry Batshaw had led a dialogue group for a time, and we were now able to revive it. There was also, within the framework of the Canadian Jewish Congress, the Cercle juif de langue française, a manifestation of the far-sighted intelligence of the executive vice-president, Saul Hayes (and of his successor, Alan Rose), directed by the great writer Naïm Kattan, who had arrived from Iraq a few years before.

One day shortly after I had become an MNA, I was invited to a luncheon at the Canadian Jewish Congress office to meet a Benedictine monk from the monastery of Saint-Benoît-du-Lac, Dom Jean-Anselme Mathys. Dom Mathys had just returned from his first trip to Israel, and he wanted to share his emotions with members of the Jewish community. He proposed a continuing dialogue, which was readily accepted, and he suggested that it be called Le Cercle de Saint-David. I had to gently point out that there were no saints in Judaism, something he did not know, and so it was named Le Cercle du Roi David. It continued for several years.

So the Canadian Council of Christians and Jews seemed an appropriate and opportune career move. I was interviewed by John Lockwood and Lou Ronson, both of whom I came to hold in high esteem. I knew something about the organization, but there was also much to discover. I had assumed that there was an active program of intellectual, theological, and historical dialogue. What I found was a feel-good program of "brotherhood" events.

The CCCJ was essentially embedded in the business community. The founding chief executive officer, the Reverend Richard Jones, would say that he went around with a book in each hand, the Bible in one and the *Directory of Directors* in the other. The annual Human Relations Award went primarily to members of the business community, many of whom were good at human relations, but some of whom were not but had been persuaded to make a significant donation.

I set out to build a genuine, in-depth dialogue program. The idea of a structured conversation between Christianity and Judaism, between Christians and Jews, was relatively recent – the CCCJ had been founded in 1947 – and the prejudice of prior centuries – the antisemitism, to give it its name – still ran deep. People did not set foot in a place of worship of another tradition. But men and women of goodwill had taken a hard look at pre–World War II Canada, had been troubled by the derogatory attitudes and words they found and by the barriers between religions, and had under-taken to do something about them.

I was enormously helped by a new senior staff person, Edith Land, who had considerable theological knowledge and was acquainted with people all across the religious spectrum. Edith was famous for the piles of paper that encumbered her office, but out of that chaos came solid programming and imaginative initiatives. She was a liaison with the Christian-Jewish Dialogue of Toronto, and I with that in Montreal and subsequently with those in other cities. The CCCJ had offices in Vancouver, Calgary, Winnipeg, Toronto, Montreal, and Halifax, with a full-time director in each, and we were an effective team.

The tradition of giving the Human Relations Award to busi-ness leaders continued – such was the board's decision – but I was able to provide another dimension as well. One year we honoured Governor General Jeanne Sauvé, with whom I had had a cordial and productive relationship when we were Ministers of the Environment, she in Ottawa and I in Quebec City. On another occasion I brought the Léger family to the podium: Governor General Jules Léger, his distinguished wife, Gabrielle, and the cardinal, Paul-Émile. (Cardinal Léger accepted with two conditions. One was that, because the event was taking place in Toronto, he had to be sure that Cardinal Emmet Carter was agreeable. The other was that he would come dressed as a simple priest. When the evening arrived, however, the two cardinals made a spectacular entrance together, both in their resplendent red robes.)

Early in my mandate, I was brought into an initiative taken jointly by the Canadian Conference of Catholic Bishops (CCCB), the Canadian Council of Churches (CCC), and the Canadian Jewish Congress (CJC). They formed a national dia-logue table, the National Tripartite Liaison Committee (NTLC) (later renamed the Canadian Christian-Jewish Consultation [CCJC]), and I was able to get the Canadian Council of Christians and Jews designated an associate member.

The NTLC was unique in the world and was much admired by other countries. The CCCB was finely represented by Bishop Eugène LaRocque of Alexandria-Cornwall in Ontario. The CCC was a less dynamic participant, taking the position that it was a coalition of churches and could not speak for its members without approval from all. (This position changed dramatically when, in later years, the CCC was represented by Heather Johnston and then by Karen Hamilton.) After a time it was decided that the individual churches be invited to the table, and the Anglican, United, Presbyterian, and Lutheran churches accepted. We were pleased to obtain representation from Orthodox Christianity as well.

Shortly after my arrival, I received a call from David Hyatt, head of the National Conference of Christians and Jews in the United States. He offered cross-border cooperation and also invited me to represent Canada in the International Council of Christians and Jews, of which he was president. Twenty-odd countries were ICCJ members (there are now more than thirty); Canada had not, until that time, been among them. In 1982 the ICCJ held its conference and annual general meeting in Berlin. David, to everyone's surprise, announced his retirement as president, and he put my name forward. I served as president of the ICCJ for eight years, until 1990.

During those eight years, the ICCJ undertook a number of significant studies, bringing together scholarly groups for each purpose. We looked at school textbooks in the different member countries, identified prejudiced and derogatory portrayals, and got each member organization to approach its country's educational authorities with the objective of having such books replaced. We similarly looked at the teaching of history, examining what – if anything – was conveyed about the minority community. We inquired into seminary education, asking what future priests and ministers were learning about Judaism and future rabbis about Christianity. We held an annual conference, in a different country each year, aiming at giving a higher profile to dialogue and fostering mutual respect.

In 1986 we met in Spain, in the historic university city of Salamanca. As we planned the conference, we came to the conclusion that we could not be in that country without taking account of its history, which included a period of coexistence between Jews, Christians, and Muslims. For the first time, we invited Muslims to join us. Nine people accepted our invitation. Muslims have participated in most of our conferences ever since. A very special person was Professor Riffat Hassan, born in Pakistan and teaching at the University of Louisville in the United States. Riffat is a Muslim feminist; she attended a number of subsequent conferences and left an impressive mark.

As the 1980s progressed, however, the perception of dialogue changed in North America. The business community, widely discriminatory in earlier years, had in more recent times brought in people of different religions and origins. When approached for funding, they now reacted by saying that there was no longer a problem. The CCCJ's income shrank, and we had to let more than half our staff go and close our regional offices. In 1987 it was mutually agreed that I should leave. I nevertheless continued to be very much involved in the Christian-Jewish Dialogue of Montreal and the Canadian Christian-Jewish Consultation. For several years in Montreal we had a Jewish-Muslim dialogue in French, and more recently we established bilateral Ukrainian-Jewish and Mormon-Jewish relations. Mutual respect and genuine friendship were, and are, very much in evidence.

Over the years, I developed a special rapport with the leadership of the Catholic Church. I was a regular attendee at the annual "Brotherhood" Dinner convened at Temple Emanu-El by Rabbi Harry Joshua Stern. That was where I met and got to know Cardinal Paul-Émile Léger. In 1972, established in Africa after his surprise resignation as archbishop of Montreal, he had opened a hospital for handicapped children – the majority poliomyelitis victims – in Yaoundé in Cameroon. He asked for the federal and Quebec governments to be represented at the opening ceremonies, and I was the minister chosen. (I was later told that it had been the cardinal's request.) The federal government was represented by Jean Chrétien, whom I met there for the first time.

Paul-Émile Léger was a force of nature. He was a pioneer of Christian-Jewish dialogue, taking vigorous initiatives well before the Second Vatican Council – where he was one of the strongest voices supporting *Nostra Aetate* during the controversial debate that preceded its adoption. (This extraordinary document cancelled out all the historical religious bases for Christian antisemitism and recognized Judaism as a living and valid religion, precursor of Christianity. It set aside all the condemnatory beliefs and attitudes which the Church had had for so many centuries against the Jews.)

The Léger foundation, especially after its formal incorporation by an act of Parliament in 1981, became a leader in promoting local management of its programs in Third World countries and in the microfinancing of women's small-scale enterprises. Cardinal Léger was for a number of years the rector (principal) of the Université de Montréal – the archbishop of Montreal automatically occupied that position – and he engineered the transition to lay leadership. (The first lay rector, Roger Gaudry, became a pillar of the cardinal's charitable endeavours.)

In 1981, back from Africa, Cardinal Léger consolidated his charitable works, those overseas and those – of increasing importance – within Quebec, into the Jules and Paul-Émile Léger Foundation, and he asked me to be one of the founding directors. From 2000 to 2003 I served as the foundation's president, stepping in at a time when there was (rare) dissension within the board and re-establishing harmony. I remain a member, and am indeed an honorary president.

The relationship with Church leadership continued during the relatively brief tenure of Cardinal Paul Grégoire (who founded the Christian-Jewish Dialogue of Montreal by instructing the Jesuit father Stéphane Valiquette to propose it to Rabbi Allan Langner) and then with Cardinal Jean-Claude Turcotte. I did an hour-long, commercial-free television program with Cardinal Turcotte, Pierre Maisonneuve's *Maisonneuve à l'écoute,* and it cemented a bond. The subject was Pope Pius XII's leadership during World War II. Cardinal Turcotte was candid about some of the negatives. I was too, but I also recalled the dramatic saving of many Italian Jews by monasteries, convents, and churches, including the Vatican itself, during that papacy. We subsequently spoke and corresponded from time to time about this and other issues.

I was president of Temple Emanu-El–Beth Sholom from 2000 to 2004. We had developed the tradition of having a speaker during the day of Yom Kippur, and in 2003 I invited Cardinal Turcotte because four decades had passed since the Second Vatican Council and the adoption by the Catholic Church of *Nostra Aetate.* He spent the whole morning on the bimah, following the service with great interest and noting the sources in Judaism of various elements of Christian worship. A moving moment came when everyone was invited to put their prayer shawl around the shoulders of the person next to them. Rabbi Leigh Lerner on one side and I on the other stood with our prayer shawls around the shoulders of Cardinal Jean-Claude Turcotte.

In 2012 I received an announcement that I would be inducted into the Papal Order of Saint Sylvester. I learned that this honour had required a personal initiative by Cardinal Turcotte and a personal decision by Pope Benedict XVI. I also learned that the Archdiocese of Montreal had never before made such a recommendation. To my knowledge, there are only three other Jewish Papal Knights; one is Sir Sigmund Sternberg of the United Kingdom and another is Rabbi David Rosen of Israel. The ceremony took place at Temple Emanu-El–Beth Sholom, and Cardinal Turcotte himself presented me with the medal and the insignia.

Christian-Jewish dialogue has been, and continues to be, a profoundly valuable undertaking. Prejudices and condemnations that have been preached and taught for almost two millennia have been set aside. The recognition that Jesus, his family, and his disciples were practising Jews and that Christianity has religious and liturgical roots in Judaism has stimulated widespread scholarly study. The conclusions of the Second Vatican Council, spelled out in *Nostra Aetate*, have been reaffirmed by every pope since John XXIII and restated explicitly by successive cardinals responsible for Catholic-Jewish relations: Edward Idris Cassidy, Walter Kasper, and Kurt Koch. One of my personal objectives has been to cause those conclusions drawn in high places to filter down to grassroots clergy and their parishioners. Protestant churches have also been regular participants in dialogue, and they have equally set aside the antisemitism of so much of Christian history.

Some churches have, however, been rather negative about the State of Israel, and this position has been a source of tensions. The vast majority of Jews throughout the world have a deep emotional attachment to Israel. They perceive it as living under constant threats to its very existence, surrounded by hostility and selectively and unfairly criticized by a variety of countries and systematically in the United Nations. They feel pride in its medical, scientific, and technological achievements and in its democratic polity, and they rise to its defence whenever it is attacked.

I am one of its defenders, notably when churches become its detractors. On two occasions the Jewish community has suspended its participation in the Canadian Christian-Jewish Consultation, and I have shared in the making and implementation of those decisions, and in the search for a resolution. I denounce the appellation of "apartheid state" as thoroughly inaccurate, and I bring forward the many positive things that Israelis do in relation to their Palestinian neighbours.

I am not unquestioning and uncritical, but I retain the idealistic vision of the state that inspired its founders. Because there are social inequalities, and sometimes injustices, I am drawn to organizations such as Rabbis for Human Rights, Doctors for Human Rights, and the New Israel Fund. I want Israel's security assured, and I hope that as it is, these imperfections will be resolved. Criticism of any government, especially a democratic one, is clearly legitimate. It is equally clear, however, that for some people anti-Israel criticism, selective and disproportionate and not matched by criticism of grave situations elsewhere in the world, has become the new antisemitism. It does not admit its name, but it is deeply troubling. And it is, sadly, especially conspicuous in the United Nations.

Outreach by both Jews and Christians, separately and together, to people of other religions is a developing initiative. In Western countries such as Canada and very particularly in Israel, many Muslims are open to conversation, although there are parts of the world where more extreme attitudes make this difficult. People of goodwill derive encouragement from each other to keep trying.

My father met the great Indian philosopher Sarvapalli Radhakrishnan, who had been professor of Oriental Religions at Oxford from 1936 to 1952 and was president of India from 1962 to 1967. He was a magnetic presence at our dinner table on two occasions, and I heard him speak several times, including his address on receiving an honorary degree from McGill. In *Recovery of Faith* he wrote the following: "In every religion today we have small minorities who are beyond the horizons of their particular faith, who believe that religious fellowship is possible, not through the imposition of any one way on the whole world but through an all-inclusive recognition that we are all searchers for the truth, pilgrims on the road, that we all aim at the same ethical and spiritual standards … The widespread existence of this state of mind is the hope of the future."

*Address to the Sixth Assembly of the World Council of Churches,*
*2 August 1983*

The World Council of Churches holds a General Assembly every seven years. The 1983 gathering took place in Vancouver, and for the first time there was active participation by representatives of non-Christian religions. In my capacity as chief

executive officer of the Canadian Council of Christians and
Jews, I was an official invitee; and as president of the International Council of Christians and Jews, I was asked to be part
of a four-person panel in a special program to which the public was invited.

One of the panel members, Dr Inamullah Khan of Pakistan,
general secretary of the World Muslim Congress, was more
influential than I and ensured that he would speak after me. I
had the feeling that he anticipated that I would devote my
speech to being simplistically supportive of Israel. I was so,
but not simplistically; and so after hearing my reflections on
peace and justice, he limited himself to exhorting the countries of the First World to be more generous and considerate
towards those of the Third.

### Peace and Justice among the Children of Abraham

Mr Moderator, Dr Khan, Sheikh Shakhirov, Reverend
Casson, ladies and gentlemen:

It is my purpose to speak of dialogue as an instrument
which may be used towards the attainment of peace and
justice.

I shall not dwell on the definition of the "children of
Abraham"; I shall assume that the title of this evening's
discussion refers to Christians, Jews and Muslims. This
requires us to disregard the fact that Abraham, Sarah,
Hagar, Ishmael and Isaac did not live alone in the world
the way Adam and Eve did; there were other people
around them, and it is possible that there are people who
today identify themselves as Jews or Muslims or Christians
who are descended from one of those other lineages.

It seems necessary that I divide my remarks into two
parts: dialogue in a context of peace, and dialogue in a
context of conflict. Immediately upon stating that intention, however, I shall tie them together with a quotation
from Martin Buber. Let me mention, in parenthesis, that
the International Council of Christians and Jews, of which

I have the honour to be the current president, has its
headquarters at Heppenheim, West Germany, in the
house in which Martin Buber lived from 1916 to 1938;
and that this year's annual I C C J Conference, which will
take place in the Netherlands in the latter part of August,
will be devoted entirely to the subject of peace.

These words of Buber's were spoken at Antwerp in July
of 1932: "We make peace, we help bring about world
peace, if we make peace wherever we are destined and
summoned to do so; in the active life of one's own community, and in that aspect of it which can actively help
determine its relationship to another community."

In one of the earliest sessions of this Assembly,
Dr Douglas Jay said something which I found particularly meaningful and moving. He said that dialogue is
not an option, but an obligation. It is an obligation
because no religion has a monopoly on love, on justice,
on the desire for peace. Even though some people sometimes invoke their religion in support and justification
of their hostile action towards someone else, I cannot
believe that the true face of any religion is one of hostility. On the contrary, the face of each religion is increasingly one of dialogue.

Let me say, with considerable insistence, that dialogue
is not a process which requires the watering down of
one's theology, of one's commitment, of one's affirma-
tion; indeed, it tends to strengthen them. It is a process
of learning, of discovery, respecting the other person's
beliefs and practices, concerns and discomforts, and
indeed that person's view and perception of his or her
self and of his or her own religion.

One of the most exciting and enriching developments
in Christian-Jewish dialogue is the privilege of sharing in
the learning experience of new Christian scholarship. It
is true that scholarship in principle has validity in its own
right, according to its inherent quality; but it is significant

in this instance that it is Christian scholarship, since it concerns a reassessment of the history of the first century of the Christian or Common Era, and a re-evaluation of interpretations on which inter-religious relations have been based for twenty centuries.

In Jewish-Muslim dialogue, I am obliged to start much farther back, from a state of much greater ignorance. Dialogue is the discovery of both similarities and differences, and an important similarity was revealed to me a few days ago by Dr Inamullah Khan; he referred to the recurrence, as a key word in the Holy Koran, of the appellation *Rachman*, the Merciful One, and it struck me forcibly that when I say Grace after Meals, there is a whole series of verses which each begin with the word *ha-Rachaman*.

Let me emphasize also that dialogue is not a path to syncretism, to an amalgamation of religions. Nor is it normally a path to joint worship, which is an exceptional undertaking to mark some special event in which we all share. Indeed, I have learned from my friend Bishop Sotirios, Greek Orthodox Bishop of Toronto, and again just yesterday from my friend the Reverend Shafik Farah, how important it is that on such occasions each should be able to express his or her own belief and commitment, not necessarily on behalf of all the participants, but necessarily in terms of his or her own theology and witness.

I turn now to the more difficult subject of dialogue in a context of conflict. I have two choices: to look backward, or to look forward: and I have chosen the second.

Let me state simply that I am a committed Jew; and that as such, I have a special attachment to that troubled land area at the eastern end of the Mediterranean, that land that is thrice holy because it is holy to each of our three religions. That attachment has three components: a spiritual, religious one; a historic one, going back to

the early chapters of the Bible; and an attachment to
the State of Israel, while not to any particular government
of that state. I have lived 25 years of my life in a world in
which there was no state of Israel; and I do not wish to
live in a world in which a state of Israel does not exist.
I remember a poem, written over forty years ago, about
Britain during the war, with enemies on one side and
the sea on the other. It is by an American poet, Alice
Duer Miller, and it is called "The White Cliffs of Dover,"
and at the end it contains the lines, "In a world where
England lies stricken and dead, I do not wish to live."
I have that kind of sentiment about the state of Israel.

I cannot deal with the subject of peace, and of dialogue
in a context of conflict, without recalling the words of
another poet, the Briton John Donne. Most of you will
be familiar with the passage beginning "No man is an
island…" It contains the lines:

Each man's death diminishes me,
For I am a part of mankind.

They are very much in my thoughts as I consider
peace and justice among the children of Abraham.

Peace will come – for the Jewish people, for the
Lebanese people, whatever their affiliation, for the
Palestinian people – when we can together mourn
every life, Muslim or Christian or Jewish, which has
been lost, and share the sadness that none of those
lives can be restored.

Peace will come when we can set aside the Lex
Talionis; when we can agree that human relations need
not be governed by Newton's Law which says that to each
action there is an equal and opposite reaction.

Peace will come when we recognize that the past can
be paralytic to the process of peace; when we can stop
quantifying the tragedies on each side and weighing
them the one against the other.

Peace will *not* come through condemnation of one
protagonist or another; nor through one-sided analyses
and interpretations of the situation past and present.

Peace will not come until we can talk to each other.

There are no simple solutions; it would be simplistic
to pretend that there are. If all the high-level discussions
have not produced them, it is unrealistic to think that we
can devise them here tonight. It is easier to define the
objectives than to identify, and implement, the means of
attaining them.

Peace requires trust; and dialogue is a means of building that trust. It also requires leadership; we cannot wait
for everyone to be ready for it.

We can talk to each other here; but there are children
of Abraham in other parts of the world who are not pres-
ently able to talk to each other. That, however, brings
me back to the words of Buber with which I began: "We
make peace, we help bring about world peace, if we make
peace wherever we are destined and summoned to do so;
in the active life of one's own community, and in that
aspect of it which can actively help determine its relationship to another community."

If we *can* talk to each other here, perhaps others can
come to talk, and to trust, through our example. If we *cannot* talk to each other here, what hope is there anywhere
else in the world?

I close with a final quotation, this one from Abraham
Lincoln. I would ask you to interpret the word *right* as
meaning the right to live in peace and justice; the word
*work* as meaning the task of bringing about peace and
justice; and the word *nation*, which Lincoln used in the
singular in 1864, in the plural. And so I come to the final
words of Lincoln's Second Inaugural Address, graven in
the Lincoln Memorial in Washington, D.C.: "With malice
toward none with charity for all; with firmness in the right,
as God gives us to see the right, let us strive on to finish
the work we are in; to bind up the nations' wounds; to

care for him who shall have borne the battle, and for his widow, and his orphan – to do all which may achieve and cherish a just and lasting peace among ourselves, and with all nations."

As Douglas Jay said, dialogue is not an option. It is an obligation. Through it, may we succeed in building trust, in generating leadership, in achieving peace.

### A Reflection on Extremism

This book was in production when the *Charlie Hebdo* massacre shocked the world, followed by a murderous hostage-taking in a Paris supermarket which was, not by coincidence, Jewish. People of goodwill, whether religiously committed or secular, have since been reflecting on how peace-seeking societies can contend with violence and hatred, and with the motivations that engender them.

Each religion says, "Ours is a religion of peace." Each religion says, "Those who invoke our religion to explain and justify violent extremism are perverting it." Each community says, "Our community should not be stigmatized and stereotyped because of this minority of extremists."

I have no wish to challenge these statements, to doubt the sincerity and goodwill of those who make them. They contain, however, an implication: We are not responsible for these people.

Of course we are not, directly. But in a broader sense, we are.

In the classic musical *South Pacific,* there is a song titled "You've Got to Be Taught to Hate." Teaching is at the root of the extremism which is de-stabilizing the world.

I must add that there are parts of the world, the Middle East in particular, where there is a significant imbalance: an imbalance of hatred, an imbalance in the *teaching* of hatred, and an imbalance in the value placed on the life of a human being.

Anger is an emotion which almost everyone feels from time to time. We hear it on open-line programs, we read it in letters to the editor, we encounter it in public and private meetings, in schools and in family relations. We feel it if we or our family or our community or our religion are made the object of hate or of ridicule. But only extremists perceive in such offences a justification for terminating the life of any human being.

Indeed, most jurisdictions in the developed world have dispensed with the death penalty, even for murder.

We cannot be passive in the face of extremism. It is not enough to say, "These people do not represent us, and their life-taking in the name of our religion is a perversion of its teachings." We must recognize that "You've Got to Be Taught to Hate." And we must take responsibility for teaching differently.

That responsibility extends to every human being, and we must teach the respect and the safeguard of the life of every human being – of both genders. I was born in an era when women's roles were preponderantly domestic. It was almost universally thought that women did not need advanced education, and that if they received it, they would be intellectually and emotionally incapable of applying it as wisely and as effectively as men. Today, the women with whom I work are every bit as capable as men in analyzing and directing the affairs of society.

There are, however, parts of the world where tradition, and yes, religion, are invoked to maintain ancient discriminations. In the name of, and for the benefit of, humanity, that needs to change. Misogyny is a crime against humanity.

Extremists are not open to dialogue; it is illusory to imagine that they could be persuaded to reasonable conversation. It is too late. Education for dialogue, for harmonious and mutually respectful coexistence, for peace, must begin early, ideally even at the preschool level. If a disease cannot be cured, we must focus on preventive medicine, on immunization.

As part of that preventive undertaking, we must look constructively at the society in which we live. We must do better in coping with poverty and undernourishment, with unemployment, with dropping out of school, and with depressing living conditions. We must root out the weeds of extremism and provide a fertile soil for personal fulfilment.

School is not the only setting in which children learn about society and about human relations. We must involve parents, and older siblings, and other family members. We must provide positive extracurricular experiences. Child and youth protection agencies, undoubtedly already sensitized, need to be assured of the resources they require. Prisons, which too often are breeding grounds for extremism, require special attention. Parole officers, and those concerned with the reinsertion of detainees into society, are important prevention agents.

We have no choice but to take up these challenges.

In the address on peace and justice which I gave to the World Council of Churches, I reached out to brothers and sisters who like me are children of Abraham. I quoted the w c c's Dr Douglas Jay: "Dialogue is not an option. It is an obligation."

So is education.

### BEHIND THE IRON CURTAIN

When I became president of the International Council of Christians and Jews and began to work with the general secretary, a Dutch Reformed Church pastor and academic named Jacobus (Coos) Schoneveld, we had occasional communications from people in Eastern Europe who gave us a slightly different portrait from the stereotypical and simplistic image of godless Communism. Coos suggested that we go and see for ourselves, and that we explore the possibility of dialogue in those countries between Christians and Jews.

The first opportunity arose in November 1980. John Rich, the British ambassador in Prague, had been consul general in Montreal in the post–October Crisis era, when the British manifested their gratitude for the rescue of James Cross by inviting Quebec ministers to cultural, diplomatic, and social events. At John and Rosemary's farewell party, when we celebrated his promotion to ambassador, he said, "If you ever come to Prague, let us know." Heading to an ICCJ executive meeting in Vienna, I stopped off in Prague. It was a very different experience from landing in Amsterdam or Zürich. Rosemary met me at the airport. With her diplomatic passport, she had been able to come through security and immigration and stand at the gate. She immediately grabbed the *International Herald Tribune* from under my arm and stuffed it in her purse, saying, "You could be in big trouble in a Communist country for bringing in a Western newspaper." I was promptly twice as apprehensive, but the unsmiling officials let me through without hesitation. We got into Rosemary's car and headed into the city.

After about fifteen minutes she turned into a residential street and pulled up beside a parked car with a young couple seated in it. She said that for anything in any way official that I wanted to do, it had to be the Canadian rather than the British embassy that shepherded me. I got into the other car. As we drove towards my pre-arranged appointment with the leadership of the Jewish community, I asked the young man if I had to assume that I should be careful in what I said because there would be "bugs" everywhere. He said, "Yes, including in this car."

We passed in front of the historic Altneuschule ("Old New Synagogue") and the clock face with twelve Hebrew letters and the hands going counter-clockwise, and pulled up in front of a four-storey greystone building. This was the "Jewish Town Hall," and I shook hands with Dr Desider Galsky, the community president, and the secretary, Artur Radwanski. They talked, and I listened and learned.

Dr Galsky told me that in the Czech part of Czechoslovakia, there had never been significant antisemitism. (The same had not been true in the Slovak area.) He himself was a historian by profession and had not previously been very active within the Jewish community. Although not a Communist sympathizer, he had been designated by the Communist government to be the community's president, and he was trying hard to fulfill that role effectively. He was seeking dialogue with the Catholic and Protestant communities, with limited success, and he welcomed the possible assistance of the ICCJ in this regard.

After a while – and a glass of kosher slivovitz, an addictive plum brandy – we set out on a walking tour of the Jewish quarter. There were eight synagogues in Prague, but only the Altneuschule and one other were still being used for worship. Three of the others had been turned into museums, one of textiles, another of silverware, and the third of religious objects. The collections were extraordinary – some years later they would travel to Montreal and other North American cities – and the reason was that Hitler, in destroying synagogues all over Europe, had collected their contents and sent them to Prague in order to create there a "Museum of Decadence." We also visited the historic cemetery, not nearly as damaged as I had expected, and next to it an exhibition of drawings and paintings by inmates, mostly children, of the Terezin (Theresienstadt) concentration camp. Finally, we went into the tiny Altneuschule and marvelled at its simplicity and its six centuries of history. (On a subsequent visit I attended Sabbath services there and had the extraordinary experience of being called up to the reading of the Torah.)

Dr Galsky delivered me back to Rosemary and John Rich. The British ambassador's residence is a magnificent house just off the Old Town Square. There is a legend that Mozart wrote one of his operas there. We had dinner, and I was jetlagged, but John and Rosemary insisted on a walk. We went down to the river and crossed the historic Charles Bridge lined with black statues. Halfway across we stopped and turned back to look up at Prague Castle. A light snow was falling, and this was one of three nights in the year when the castle was illuminated, and it was absolute fairyland. Then I understood why John and Rosemary had insisted on the walk. It was the only way that they could get away from the microphones picking up their every word in their home, and talk freely.

Before I left, I had one extraordinary encounter. Somehow, I had been allowed to have an appointment with Cardinal Frantiszek Tomaszek, the head of the Catholic Church in Czechoslovakia. He was over ninety, living almost alone in the large Archbishop's Palace just outside the gates of Prague Castle, and he was waging a lonely battle against the Communist regime. Ten of the fourteen sees in Czechoslovakia were without bishops, because the government would reject the cardinal's nominees and he, with the Vatican's support, would reject the fellow-travellers put forward by the regime. He was an impressive man, and I wished I could have been of some help.

The ICCJ had its headquarters in Heppenheim, a small city south of Frankfurt and north of Heidelberg, in the house which from 1922 to 1938 had been the home of the great Jewish philosopher Martin Buber. Buber had settled there because it was about equidistant between the two universities at which he taught. After his urgent departure for Israel (still Palestine in those days) in 1938, the house was given over to various uses and eventually became vacant. The government then donated it rent-free to the ICCJ, on the condition that the organization become part of the local community and offer conferences, lectures, and educational activities.

It was in Heppenheim that the ICCJ held its 1981 annual conference and meeting. I had not been in Germany for half a century, and I was intensely uncomfortable at the idea of setting foot on German soil; but I felt an obligation to the organization and forced myself to go. I met so many people of obvious sincerity and desire for collective redemption, and of deep commitment to Christian-Jewish relations, that I came to feel more positively. The next time I had to go, I urged Sheila to come with me. She had the same resistance, but she ultimately accepted and came to share my positive perceptions. When the Heppenheim meeting was convened, I was able to arrange for Desider Galsky and Artur Radwanski to get exit visas in order to attend, and we began building the ICCJ behind the Iron Curtain.

In 1982 the conference was in Berlin. We were of course in the western half of the city, but Coos Schoneveld was able to arrange for us to spend a day in East Berlin. We met with the Jewish, Catholic, and Protestant communities, walked on Unter den Linden, visited the extraordinary Pergamon Museum, and said Kaddish at the grave of Moses Mendelssohn, celebrated philosopher, pioneer of Jewish-Christian dialogue, and grandfather of the composer.

I made several subsequent trips to East Berlin, and members of its Jewish community were able to attend ICCJ meetings. A special friendship developed with Stefan Schreiner, a Protestant who taught Jewish studies at Humboldt University in that city – later at the University of Tübingen in the West – and who became a stalwart of the ICCJ.

On more than one occasion, I attended services in an East Berlin synagogue. They were led, in the absence of a rabbi, by Cantor Oljean Ingster, with whom I developed a warm relationship. The congregation of about thirty people, almost entirely male, comprised a handful of German Jews who had managed somehow to survive in hiding, and a majority of people from Poland who, despite the constraints of life in East Germany, found that country a little more welcoming and less antisemitic than their own – although Poland was already changing and would make considerable progress when Communism disappeared.

Our next initiative was in Hungary. Coos Schoneveld made contact with the Reformed Church, and Bishop Tibor Bartha invited us to be their guests. I was asked to speak at a Sunday morning service in downtown Budapest. The 350 seats were full, and I learned that they had three services each Sunday to accommodate the faithful. A university professor kindly translated my words. I was necessarily careful in what I said, but I spoke about human relations across the dividing lines of religious difference, and about the ICCJ as an international agent for peace and understanding.

The Jewish community in Hungary, after World War II and the Holocaust, was the largest in Eastern Europe outside the Soviet Union, and it had the only rabbinical academy east of the Iron Curtain, training rabbis for all the Communist countries. The head, Rabbi Sandor Scheiber, was a man of impressive intellect and appealing personality. The academy had an exceptional library, and Rabbi Scheiber let us hold a book that he said had been owned by Maimonides and brought to Hungary when the Jews were expelled from Spain in 1492. Rabbi Scheiber and two or three colleagues were subsequently able to attend ICCJ conferences, as was a young Reformed Church minister named Bertalan Tamas, who spoke excellent English because he had benefited from a Reformed Church exchange program with the Church of Scotland.

We turned then to Poland. The Holocaust had virtually annihilated its pre-war Jewish population of 3,300,000 people, but we established a long-standing relationship with a young man named Stanislaw Krajewski, who had succeeded in starting a Catholic-Jewish dialogue. He and his wife, Monika, a photographer, were also involved in documenting, preserving, and restoring Jewish historic sites, primarily cemeteries but also community buildings. I met a Catholic priest, Father Stanislaw Musial (pronounced "Mushau" in Polish), who was very much aware of a famous American baseball player of the same name and who was actively devoted to dialogue and understanding.

The Communist regime was strong and in control, but there was stalwart resistance by the Catholic Church and by an intellectual movement centred on a publication called *Tygodnyk Powsechny*. We met its publisher, Jerzy Turowicz, and his colleague Stefan Wilkanowicz; we were profoundly impressed by their intelligence, and by their courage in publishing essays and articles of a high intellectual level that challenged the Communist ideology.

This was the time of the crisis over the Carmelite convent at Auschwitz. A community of Carmelites, cloistered nuns devoted to prayer, had settled into a building just outside the wall of the concentration camp. It had originally been a theatre, but the Nazis had used it as a storage facility for the lethal gas employed in the extermination buildings. Jewish communities throughout the world reacted intensely. Ultimately, with the personal intervention of Pope John Paul II (Karol Wojtyła), the nuns would be moved to a new complex built some distance away, but at the time of my visit they were still very much there.

In my capacity as president of the ICCJ, I had written a polite but deeply concerned letter about the Carmelite problem to the archbishop of Cracow, Cardinal Macharski, in whose archdiocese Auschwitz is situated. He met me at the gate of the camp, and we went through both Auschwitz and Birkenau together. He then drove me to his residence in Cracow, speaking French because he was more fluent in that language than in English. His concern was clearly genuine, and he kept thanking me for mine. He was not perceived as a strong figure in the Catholic hierarchy, but I felt admiration and affection for him.

We in the West had an image of the Communist regimes as suppressive of religions and of political opposition. What I found on the ground was appreciably different. Religions were hampered and harassed, but they were surviving. There *was* an opposition, and it was easy to be a part of it – join a church. Christian-Jewish dialogue began on a small scale in each of these countries and slowly grew. Each had contact with the ICCJ, and when the Iron Curtain came down, they became full members.

## A MEETING WITH THE POPE

In July 1984 the ICCJ held its annual conference in Italy, in the hill town of Vallombrosa-Saltino, above Florence. For a number of years we had had a Vatican observer and liaison as a member of our executive, and through Father Jorge Mejia (later bishop and cardinal), we were able to obtain an audience with the Pope.

Sixteen of us gathered in St Peter's Square. Well before the appointed hour, we approached a door in the building to the right of the great church. The Swiss Guards passed us through, and Vatican officials led us up an impressive staircase and into a room with a throne of stone, slightly elevated and with minimal decoration. We were counted, and chairs were removed so that there were exactly sixteen. We learned that there must not be an empty chair at a papal audience. As we took our seats, we were informed that the Pope was devoting that morning to a considerable series of audiences, and that when he reached us, he might not be still on schedule. If he was running late, he would limit the encounter to hearing our address and responding to it; but if he was on time, he would remain afterwards and converse with us. We were fortunate.

Even though we knew that John Paul II was a charismatic human being and an exceptional communicator, we were unprepared for the impact of his personality. He took his seat on the throne, and I stood and addressed him. Monsignor Mejia had prepared us meticulously and had required the text of my remarks in advance so that the Pope could respond appropriately. I spoke about dialogue, about the progress it had made in recent years, and about the new impetus given it by the Second Vatican Council. I asked the Pope to provide leadership in sustaining it and helping it to advance.

John Paul listened intently and responded in kind. He described our work as important and encouraged us to continue involving young people in it. He referred to *Nostra Aetate* and thanked us for contributing to world peace. Then he stepped down from the throne, relaxed visibly, smiled, and went around the room shaking hands with each individual. He spent a good deal of time conversing with us, eschewing the superficial and responding cogently to our comments and questions. He was interested in where each of us came from and what had motivated us to become involved in dialogue – and he thanked us for it.

One rather special thing happened. We had been told that the formal dress code for a papal audience had been discontinued and that only shorts and sleeveless shirts were prohibited. One of our number, however, Claire Huchet-Bishop of France, no longer young, had dressed in the old-fashioned way: a formal black dress, long gloves, and a black lace covering on her head. This was clearly a pious Catholic, meeting the head of her church.

When the Pope reached her, she exerted the privilege of age and did not let go of his hand. She looked him in the eyes, spoke about the nature of dialogue, and ended by saying to him, "And so, Your Holiness, you *have* to give diplomatic recognition to the State of Israel." John Paul responded cordially; he obviously was not able to make that commitment at that time, but his words were not negative, and the recognition indeed followed some years later.

Knowing that the Pope had had quite a number of audiences that day, we were greatly and pleasantly surprised that we were the leading front-page article of the next morning's *Osservatore Romano*. The full texts of our address and the Pope's response are included in the 2011 book compiled and edited by Dr Eugene J. Fisher and the late Rabbi Leon Klenicki, *The Saint for Shalom: How Pope John Paul II Transformed Catholic-Jewish Relations*.

*Address to the Pope from the International Council of Christians and Jews, 6 July 1984*

Your Holiness,

In expressing the gratitude of the International Council of Christians and Jews for the privilege of this audience, I would like to say an introductory word to identify the ICCJ. It has existed for a considerable number of years in somewhat various forms. At present it is composed of seventeen national member organizations, all in the Western World; but it is significant that in the last four years we have been able to bring to our meetings a number of people, Christians and Jews, from Eastern Europe: from Czechoslovakia, from East Germany and from Hungary.

If we continue to meet, year after year, in this fashion, it is because of the friendship, the understanding and the trust which continue to grow between us. It is also because antisemitism, and other forms of hatred, including anti-Catholicism, are still unfortunately present in the world. But it is also because we share a sense of historic opportunity, the opportunity to set aside the antagonisms of the past and live together in peace.

For some years now, notably since (and as a result of) the Second Vatican Council, we have been experiencing a new era in Christian-Jewish relations, an era of undeniable progress.

Jews and Christians alike have reason to be grateful for the leadership which the Church has given in this work, leadership manifested by yourself and your recent predecessors; by Cardinal Bea; by Cardinal Willebrands; by Cardinal Etchegaray, whose remarkable statement we regard as a landmark and a beacon; by Monsignor Jorge Mejia, whose attendance at ICCJ meetings is greatly appreciated and whose intellectual contributions to our work are exceptionally valuable; by Dr. Eugene Fisher, both administratively and educationally; and by many others.

It has been a reciprocal learning process, and one of the most significant lessons we have derived from it is that the growth of harmony, understanding and mutual respect has in no way diminished the religious integrity and vitality of Judaism or of Christianity – quite the contrary – nor weakened the commitment of any Jew or of any Christian to his or her faith and tradition.

What is deeply appreciated is the readiness of the
Church, under your leadership, to review liturgy, to
revise catechism, to reassess and reinterpret history,
to recognize that teachings and policies in the past
have erected barriers and indeed led to persecutions.

What is also deeply appreciated is the sense of mutual
respect and equal partnership which pervades today's
relationships.

Our dialogue has become not only a conversation about
Judaism and Christianity, about Jews and Christians, but
also a sharing of common concerns: *for* peace, *against*
violence, *against* fanaticism, *against* curtailment of
human rights and religious freedoms, *against* injustice
and inequality and discrimination, *for* cooperation and
decency and human dignity. Christian-Jewish dialogue is
building a foundation for working together on behalf of
humanity.

Our concern for peace extends throughout the world; it
has a particular focus on the Middle East. We mourn every
life that has been lost, Christian or Jewish or Muslim; and
we pray that the State of Israel and its neighbours may
come to live in security, in recognition, and in fruitful
rather than hostile relations. We invoke your leadership
towards these ends.

We renew our gratitude for the privilege of this audience. Knowing you at a distance, we have admired your
courageous initiatives and have valued your contributions to Christian-Jewish understanding. Meeting you
now in person, we take encouragement from you in the
continuation of our work.

That encouragement emboldens us to express a
particular hope. We submit with respect, and with great
appreciation for the statements you have made and
the positions you have taken, that it is not enough for
pronouncements to be made at the highest level; they
must be heard and heeded in every parish as well.

We ask you therefore to continue the leadership
you have manifested in Christian-Jewish relations. We
ask you, in so doing, to reinforce the work of the Vatican
Commission on Relations with the Jews; to upgrade the
commission; to give it more scope, initiative and authority.
We also hope earnestly for the day when every diocese will
have a person responsible for the dissemination of new
understanding among its clergy and laity, for liaison with
the Jewish community wherever it exists, in the State of
Israel and throughout the world, and for the educational
and practical implementation, at the grassroots level, of
the statements and positions and decisions which derive
from your initiative.

For all of this, we ask God's blessing upon you.

### The Pope's Response

(The headline in the Vatican newspaper read: "The Pope to
the International Council of Christians and Jews: The peace
of the world must be built through the elimination of prejudice and the pursuit of dialogue.")

Dear Friends, Mr President, and Members of the
Executive Committee of the International Council of
Christians and Jews:

I thank you, Mr President, for the kind words of greeting with which you have now presented to me the aims,
the tasks and the concerns of the International Council
of Christians and Jews. And I thank you also, members
of the Executive Committee, for your kindness in visiting
the Pope on the occasion of your international collo-
quium, to be held at Vallombrosa next week. Welcome
to this house where the activities of those who promote
the dialogue between Christians and Jews and are personally engaged in it are closely followed and warmly
encouraged. Indeed, it is only through such a meeting of
minds and hearts, reaching out to our respective faith

communities, and also perhaps to other faith communities, as you try to do with Islam, that both Jews and
Christians are able to profit from their "great common
spiritual patrimony" (*Nostra Aetate,* 4) and to make it
fruitful for their own good and the good of the world.

Yes, a "great common spiritual patrimony" which
should be, in the first place, brought to the knowledge
of all Christians and all Jews and which embraces not
only one or the other isolated element but a solid, fruitful, rich common religious inheritance in monotheism;
in faith in a God who as loving father takes care of
humankind and chose Abraham and the Prophets and
sent Jesus into the world; in a common basic liturgical
pattern and in a common consciousness of our commitment, grounded in faith, to all men and women in need,
who are our "neighbours" (Leviticus 19:18a, Mark 12:32,
and parallels).

This is why you are so much concerned with religious
education on both sides, that the images which each of us
projects of the other should be really free of stereotypes
and prejudices, that they should respect the other's identity, and should in fact prepare the people for the meetings of minds and hearts just mentioned. The proper
teaching of history is also a concern of yours. Such a concern is very understandable, given the sad and entangled
common history of Jews and Christians – a sad history
which is not always taught or transmitted correctly.

There is again the danger of an always active and sometimes even resurgent tendency to discriminate between
people and human groups, enhancing some and despis-
ing others, a tendency which does not hesitate at times to
use violent methods.

To single out and denounce such facts and stand
together against them is a noble act and a proof of our
mutual brotherly commitment. But it is necessary to go
to the roots of such evil, by education, especially

education for dialogue. This, however, would not be enough if it were not coupled with a deep change in our heart, a real spiritual conversion. This also means constantly reaffirming common religious values and working toward a personal religious commitment in the love of God, our Father, and in the love of all men and women (Deuteronomy 6:5, Leviticus 19:18, Mark 12:28-34). The Golden Rule, we are well aware, is common to Jews and Christians alike.

In this context is to be seen your important work with youth. By bringing together young Christians and Jews, and enabling them to live, talk, sing and pray together, you greatly contribute toward the creation of a new generation of men and women, mutually concerned for one another and for all, prepared to serve others in need, whatever their religious profession, ethnic origin or colour.

World peace is built in this modest, apparently insignificant and limited, but in the end, very efficient, way. And we are all concerned for peace everywhere, among and within nations, particularly in the Middle East.

Common study of our religious sources is again one of the items of your agenda. I encourage you to put to good use the important recommendation made by the Second Vatican Council in its declaration *Nostra Aetate*, 4, about "biblical and theological studies," which are the source of "mutual understanding and respect." In fact, such studies, made in common, and altogether different from the ancient "disputation," tend to the true knowledge of each religion, and also to the joyful discovery of the "common patrimony" I spoke of at the beginning, always in the careful observance of each other's dignity.

May God bless all your endeavours and repay you with the blessedness which Jesus proclaimed, in the tradition of the Hebrew Scriptures, for those who work for peace (Matthew 5:9, Psalm 37 (36):37).

# Transitions, 1987–1991

By the fall of 1987, it seemed time for me to leave the Canadian Council of Christians and Jews. Feeling far from ready to retire, I turned to the Government of Quebec. Robert Bourassa had returned from the wilderness and recaptured the leadership of the Quebec Liberal Party, leading it to electoral victory. He was welcoming. Clifford Lincoln was the Minister of the Environment. I had never met him, but I knew of his top-notch reputation. The presidency of the Environmental Public Hearings Board, universally known by its French acronym, BAPE, was vacant. A meeting was arranged, we hit it off extremely well, and he offered me the job.

The law required that for major projects of a wide range of types, an environmental-impact study had to be carried out and made public, and the BAPE went to that part of the province to hold public hearings, which allowed the local citizens to listen to the promoter's presentation and come to the microphone to express their opinions. It was an exhilarating experience in direct democracy. The ultimate decision was in the hands of the minister and the cabinet, but the BAPE was often in a position to identify significant environmental hazards and make constructive proposals for change.

The BAPE rated highly in public opinion and in the media. Clifford Lincoln was totally supportive, and other ministers, although sometimes less than happy with our conclusions, treated us with respect. One in particular, Marc-Yvan Côté, had numerous projects for roads and other constructions, and we often identified problems that required revision; but he was consistently understanding and supportive. Public preoccupation with the protection of the environment was much higher and much better informed than it had been seventeen years before.

Some two years went rewardingly by, and the work of the BAPE was going smoothly, but then a dramatic – indeed, historic – event intervened. Robert Bourassa, preoccupied, as he had been in 1974, with the protection of the French language, but not skilled in relating to the English-speaking community, chose to invoke the "notwithstanding clause" in the Canadian Charter of Rights and Freedoms in order to override a decision by the Supreme Court of Canada that it was acceptable to require French on commercial signs, in a larger type size than other languages, but that it was a violation of freedom of expression to ban English and other tongues. When the vote came, Clifford Lincoln made his historic speech – "Rights are rights are rights, and always will be rights" – and he, Herbert Marx, and Richard French resigned from the cabinet .

Lise Bacon became the new Minister of the Environment. I had had a good relationship with her for many years – she had been president of the party during my years as an opposition MNA, and we had had many constructive conversations – but now there was a palpable coldness. The BAPE had been handed a major issue, the safe management of hazardous wastes, and I wrote her an internal communication to say that we needed to find a balance between informing the public and provoking anxiety. A few days later I woke up to find my letter on the front page of *Le Devoir* with a calumnious insinuation that I did not want the public to be adequately informed. Lise, instead of supporting me, used this as a pretext to ask me to leave. It was Marc-Yvan Côté who recognized the injustice, and the ingratitude to a person with a long and significant record of public service; he also saw that public opinion was reacting very negatively to Lise's action, and he set out to find me another position. He had meanwhile become Minister of Health, and he named me executive director of the Quebec Health Research Foundation (F R S Q).

I had been a practising pediatrician, not a research scientist, but this appointment proved to be a gratifying challenge. I acquired a warm new friendship: the president was Dr Patrick Vinay, a kidney specialist who subsequently became dean of Medicine at the Université de Montréal and ultimately a specialist in palliative care. Patrick was a person of great intellect and profound human sensitivity. We formed a harmonious team, and he helped me get to know a world which had been peripheral to my earlier experience but which I knew was fundamental to the progress of medical knowledge and of patient care.

Then, one day in June 1991, my phone rang. It was the prime minister of Canada, Brian Mulroney, and he was calling to offer me the position of Commissioner of Official Languages. Marc-Yvan Côté put me even more deeply in his debt by unhesitatingly waiving the three-month notice in my F R S Q contract. I became an officer of the Parliament of Canada.

# Official Languages, 1991–1999

## COMMISSIONER

The Commissioner of Official Languages is named, not by cabinet order-in-council (essentially by the prime minister), but by a vote of the House of Commons and the Senate. He or she is therefore politically non-partisan and has seven years of tenure. The position was created in 1969 with the adoption of the first Official Languages Act. Keith Spicer was the first commissioner, taking office in 1970. Max Yalden was next and then d'Iberville Fortier. I was succeeded by Dyane Adam; Graham Fraser followed.

It was unseemly to campaign for the position, but necessary to make one's interest known. I learned that the dossier was piloted by the Secretary of State. I knew Gilles Loiselle only slightly, but well enough to ask for a conversation, which took place in his Quebec City office. He was of course non-committal, but he did go so far as to say that mine was a quality candidacy. Prime Minister Brian Mulroney and I knew each other. He spoke very effective French, and official languages were important to him. I had not, since 1965, been active in federal politics – and federal Conservatives in those days were generally provincial Liberals. In any case he clearly placed the choice of commissioner above political partisanship.

When I took office, I asked myself why I had been chosen. Being fluently bilingual was a necessary factor, as well as having a fair knowledge of Canada from coast to coast, but I had to conclude that my political experience had been the determinant, and that I needed to assess public perceptions of official languages and to act accordingly. My sense that public opinion was widely negative took no time to be confirmed. In the nine provinces and (then) two territories where English was the majority language, the law was widely perceived as a coercive imposition, making French unnecessarily conspicuous and requiring so many federal public servants to be bilingual that unilingual English-speakers were discriminated against. In Quebec, although the Official Languages Act was seen as important by the English-speaking minority, it was viewed among the majority population as competitive with Bill 101, the Charter of the French Language, and of little significance in the life of the province. I also perceived a cleavage between opinion leaders and grassroots citizens. Many of the former understood Canada's linguistic duality and were supportive of it; large numbers of the latter had negative opinions of its purposes and applications.

I took up the challenge. Each morning I received a substantial sheaf of press clippings from all across the country, covering both the major daily newspapers and a host of regional and local dailies and weeklies. Included were not only articles and editorials, but – most valuably – letters to the editor. Those letters were in large majority negative and very often filled with wrong information and wild assertions, and I promptly sat down at my computer and fired off a detailed reply to every single one that required it. Editorials, however, especially in the major dailies, were almost uniformly positive, and when I set out early on to travel across the country, I met with editorial boards, who naturally subjected me to provocative questioning but were thoroughly supportive.

Television and radio were means of communicating with large numbers of people, and official-language controversies made them very much interested. There were one or more open-line radio programs in every city, with hosts who were occasionally sympathetic but more often sceptical or downright hostile – as were their callers – and I did dozens of such programs in every province and territory. I met with premiers, ministers of education, and ministers of justice, as well as with senior public servants. In a few instances, there was also a minister responsible for French-language services. Although an occasional person was unreceptive, the conversations were generally constructive.

I also sought speaking engagements wherever I went and was welcomed by Rotary Clubs everywhere and by some Canadian Clubs, Kiwanis Clubs, and Knights of Columbus. These were very positive experiences. I found that the large majority of members came to these encounters with an open-minded interest in what the speaker had to say, and that their community commitment made them draw constructive and socially responsible conclusions.

All was not negative therefore – indeed, there was significant positive support, notably from an organization called Canadian Parents for French. Present in every province and territory, these English-speaking parents (with, of course, a variety of mother tongues), many not themselves fluent in French, were committed to their children learning that language and being thus able to participate more fully in Canada. Immersion programs in schools were the method of choice.

French immersion had been introduced in the 1970s and grew slowly at first. In the 1980s its popularity mushroomed, and when I became commissioner there were some 300,000 non-French-speaking Canadian children enrolled. I wondered if that number would peak and fall off, if other priorities would take over, but that did not happen. That had to mean that year after year, when one cohort of children graduated and another entered school, the word of mouth from the first set of parents to the second was "This was a great experience for my child and I really recommend it for yours." Obviously, not all these children became or remained fully bilingual. Maintaining fluency requires continuing exposure, continuing opportunities to use the language. The sensitization to the reality of Canada's linguistic duality is invaluable, however, and if as adults these young people are in positions of leadership, it will be easier for them to recapture that linguistic ability.

There is a semantic distinction that needs to be made. Canada is not a bilingual country. We are a country with two official languages. Our federal institutions offer services and information to Canadian citizens *where numbers warrant*. Most positions, and most offices, in the federal public service – about two-thirds of them – are *not* designated bilingual. The offices that are have a sign identifying them as such.

The Commissioner of Official Languages is a member of the Canadian Association of Ombudsmen. He or she receives complaints from Canadian citizens who have not obtained service or information in their preferred official language from a federal office or public servant. In keeping with my preoccupation with public opinion, I attached great importance to this function and worked to ensure the efficiency of our complaint handling. The feedback we received from Canadian citizens was predominantly positive.

In each province and territory, there is an organized official-language minority community. Although I devoted great effort to educating the majorities, I learned early on how much the minorities count on the commissioner's support. I essentially visited each province each year – it was logistically difficult to be as regular a presence in the territories – and I made a point of sitting down with the minority community leadership, taking note of their problems, working with them on solutions, and when possible meeting with their general membership.

A major issue for them all was school governance. When I started in 1991, only New Brunswick and Prince Edward Island had created a French-language school board structure. (Quebec, which had long had Protestant and Catholic school boards, changed them in 1993 to English and French.) When I left in 1999, all nine English-majority provinces and both territories had done so. In several instances, the change had required court action, and I had vigorously and pragmatically supported each and every case. School governance was important because without it French-language schools were bound by the priorities and policies of the majority and could not determine their own. As well, the allocation of resources was sometimes parsimonious and hamstringing.

A resource that the French-language minority communities found valuable was the combined school and community centre. In 1991 there were only five in all of Canada, but by 1999 there were fifteen, and others were on the drawing board. Parents bringing their children to school or calling for them at the end of the day, and of course other adults, adolescents, and senior citizens as well, could find cultural or athletic programs of interest in the adjacent, generally attached, community centre, and this resource enhanced community vitality.

The English-speaking community in Quebec lived (and continues to live) with a particular set of problems. No longer the dominant economic force, it has recognized the existential concerns of its French-speaking fellow citizens and has gained conspicuous skill in communicating in French. Nevertheless, it – rather than the English language itself – is still perceived by some as a negative and even hostile factor in Quebec society. I have vigorously contested that perception. During my years as commissioner, I spent time with the Townshippers and communities in the Gaspé, the Outaouais, the Saint-Maurice valley, and elsewhere, and met with Premier Robert Bourassa and successive ministers of education – including Claude Ryan – and with English-speaking MNAs. Headway was elusive. Moral support to the community was appreciated by its members, but it had limited impact on Quebec's linguistic preoccupations.

I left office with the feeling that ill-informed letters to the editor had diminished, that federal institutions were a little more responsive, and that Canada was a little more comfortable in its two-languages skin – and would no longer accept a federal political leader who could not speak both languages.

Shortly before the end of my mandate, I was in the Jean Lesage Airport in Quebec City, and in the check-in area I spotted Gilles Vigneault. I hardly thought he would know who I was, but he made a beeline for me, shook my hand, and thanked me rather emotionally for all I was doing for the French language and for French-speakers throughout Canada. I was rather emotional in thanking him.

Towards the end of my term, an issue had arisen in Ottawa with regard to health care in French. It had two components. One concerned the amalgamation of the two major hospitals, the General and the Civic. The other was a proposal to close the Montfort. The Civic was essentially an English-speaking hospital. The General was bilingual and attracted a substantial French-speaking clientele. It was obvious, however, that in the merged entity, French-speaking patients – and French-speaking staff – would be in the minority, and that unless a clear and pragmatic policy was established and effectively implemented, patients and their families could not be assured of being cared for in French.

I went to see the executive director of the merged institution, David Levine. He had arrived a year or so before, in a storm of controversy because he had been a Parti Québécois candidate (in D'Arcy McGee, although not against me) and was still very much identified with the party. There was widespread and emotional criticism of a separatist being named to head the principal hospital in Canada's capital. I did not know David at that time. (Some years later he would be named by a Parti Québécois government to head the Montreal Health and Social Services Agency, and I was chairperson of the board throughout his tenure.) He committed himself to a positive language policy, and his board gave him its full backing.

The Montfort Hospital was a more difficult problem. Medium-sized, it was seen as expendable by health care planners. It was, however, the only French-speaking hospital in the Ottawa area, and it served the substantial French-speaking population of Eastern Ontario (where the only other resource was a small institution in Hawkesbury). A grassroots preservation movement sprang up, and I became actively involved in it.

I worked with its president, Gisèle Lalonde, and was very much in the media on the issue. Member of Parliament Mauril Bélanger lent his weight to the effort, and federal Health Minister Allan Rock became interested. I worked with the dean of Medicine at the University of Ottawa, Peter Walker; and with the federal government providing the funds, we made the Montfort into a teaching hospital to train French-speaking health care professionals for the minority communities all across Canada. Subsequently, the Association des médecins de langue française du Canada (now Médecins francophones du Canada) awarded Gisèle Lalonde and myself its Centennial Medal.

The issue of language as a therapeutic instrument has been a major one for English-speaking Quebecers as well as for French-speaking minority communities. I have constantly pointed out that an accurate diagnosis depends on the patient conveying the precise and detailed nature of his or her symptoms; he or she may be reasonably good in a second language, but may not have all the necessary vocabulary or ease of expression. One is usually stressed in the face of illness and may therefore not be as articulate as usual. Also, follow-up care requires the patient's clear understanding of the physician's instructions, and language may be a factor there as well. I have always put these issues in human rather than legalistic terms.

## DON GETTY ACROSS THE LINE OF SCRIMMAGE

I was barely six months into my mandate when I learned that Premier Don Getty of Alberta had denounced "forced bilingualism" in an address to the Rotary Club of Edmonton.

Coming from so well-regarded a public figure, this was a matter of particularly serious concern. My Commissioner's Representative for Western Canada, Deni Lorieau, who was based in Edmonton and knew the Rotary leadership, found that the club was without a speaker for its regular meeting three weeks later and got me the slot.

I had met Don Getty some years before, when we were both provincial cabinet ministers. I had, of course, known him through the media as one of Canada's outstanding football players, and in person he came across as intelligent and thoroughly decent. I knew that in making that speech he was reflecting public opinion in his province – and that he was seriously uninformed.

I always had a small, transient flutter of anxiety whenever I got up to speak, but Daniel in the lions' den could not have been more apprehensive than I was as I arrived in Edmonton. My experience with Rotary Clubs, however, had always been positive, and continued to be so throughout my term. I found their members civic-minded and socially conscientious, and they welcomed a wide variety of speakers with genuine interest in what each had to say. They showed their decency in spades on this occasion.

Usually I speak spontaneously, but this was a time when a prepared text was essential. It was a bit longer than the club might have wished, but everyone listened attentively and no one walked out. The question period was cordial and sensible, and the chairperson made no attempt to curtail it. The warmth was striking. The last question was a request: that I tell Quebecers how much regard Albertans had for them. More than one journalist commented on a conspicuous paradox. Don Getty had received a standing ovation. So did I.

After the speech I was ushered into an adjacent room where some twenty journalists were gathered. They were, predictably, a good deal more aggressive than the Rotarians had been, and they tried hard to get me to say that I had come to Edmonton to pick a fight with Don Getty. I resisted that interpretation, spoke of my regard for the premier, and insisted that I had simply wanted to get the facts on the record. Their appetite for conflict was unsatisfied, but their reporting afterwards was objective and fair.

*Address to the Downtown Edmonton Rotary Club, 30 January 1992*

I estimate that in the course of my career I must have given over 2,000 speeches. I consider that this is one of the most important, and I thank you for giving me the opportunity to deliver it.

I would ask you to receive it in one context and one context only, that of the unity of our country.

I am not a polemicist, a person whose style is aggressive and controversial – not only because polemic is not part of my nature, but also because a country cannot be built on bitterness. I want to contribute to improving, to healing the climate in which we are carrying on our discussion about Canada's future.

I would like to examine with you what the law, Canada's Official Languages Act, does and does not say; what impact the law has on Alberta and on Albertans; what the Commissioner of Official Languages does and does not do; and what this particular Commissioner of Official Languages is trying to achieve. In the last part of my speech, I would like to reflect with you on some historical considerations, on what history, I hope, may be able to teach us.

The Official Languages Act is not about compulsion; it is about service to the public, about fairness to Canadian citizens. There is nothing in it about shoving French down the throats of English-speaking Canadians. On the contrary, it embodies the right of an English-speaking Canadian, especially one living in a majority situation, to be and remain a unilingual English-speaking Canadian. The same principle applies to the French-speaking

Canadian. It is precisely because each has the right to
be unilingual that the government of Canada is called
upon to provide services to the citizens of this country
in two languages.

It is not the purpose of the Act to make Canada uniformly, homogeneously bilingual from sea to sea to sea.
The objective is to make federal services available in
both languages, and that only where concentrations
of population justify it, where significant demand is
demonstrated. Regulations have just been promulgated
to establish criteria for the provision of these services.
Incidentally, Alberta MPs made constructive contributions to the development of these regulations, and a
number of their proposals are incorporated in them.

In communities where services in two languages are
needed, there have to be people to provide them. In
Alberta, out of 2,400,000 people, about 400 federal public servants (out of 13,000) are required to be bilingual
in order to be able to serve French-speaking Albertans
where their communities are large enough. The R C M P
has over 2,000 officers and constables in Alberta; 105 of
those positions are designated bilingual. Crown corpora-
tions have small numbers of bilingual positions. Everyone
else is free to be unilingual English. Incidentally, out of
2,400,000 people in this province, about 80,000 English-
speaking Albertans identify themselves as also speaking
French. This is hardly a picture of compulsion.

Those 400 public servants in Alberta represent 3% of
the total. 97% of federal public service jobs in Alberta
are open to unilingual English-speaking people, and that
includes 90% of management-level positions. There are
87 management-level positions in Alberta; nine of them
are bilingual posts, and eight out of the nine are held by
English-speaking Albertans. Overall, there are no bilingual positions in Lethbridge, none in Medicine Hat,
one in Grande Prairie, two in Peace River, two in Fort

McMurray, four in Red Deer, thirteen in Jasper, 81 in all of Calgary and 252 in Edmonton.

The same is true all across Western Canada. With 7,300,000 total population and about 50,000 federal public servants, there are only 1,600 bilingual jobs, 3% of the total.

What about Canada's population as a whole? Out of 26,000,000 Canadians, about 6,500,000 are French-speaking, 4,000,000 of them speaking French only. 4,000,000 Canadians are able to speak both languages. 18,000,000 Canadians speak English only. Only 1.2% of Canadians are unable to speak either English or French. Only 7% of Canadians, a figure stable since 1971, use a language other than English or French at home.

With English *and* French, then, we reach 98.8% of Canadians. No other language allows us to reach more than 2% of Canada's population. When Canadians were asked, in the 1986 census, to identify their heritage language, 554,000 gave Italian, 527,000 German, 309,000 Chinese and 277,000 Ukrainian. All others were below 200,000.

Incidentally, eleven languages in the world are spoken by more than 100,000,000 people each. French is one of them, at 119,000,000 in 33 countries. English, of course, is another, at 437,000,000 in some fifty countries.

Incidentally also, let me remind you that the teaching of French is not compulsory in Alberta schools. Each school board decides what it wishes to do in this regard.

A million French-speaking Canadians, a number equivalent to the total population of Manitoba or Saskatchewan, live outside Quebec. About a million people in Quebec are English-speaking, two-thirds of them by mother tongue. About two million Canadians depend, therefore, on our Official Languages system for appropriate service from federal departments and institutions.

Is Canada's official languages policy a plot to favour Francophones over Anglophones? The answer is no, absolutely not – neither in its intent, nor in its results. Although bilingual Francophones may be a little easier to find than bilingual Anglophones, 61% of the bilingual federal public service jobs in Alberta and 63% of those in the four Western provinces are held by Anglophones. In Canada as a whole, the percentage of Francophones in federal public service positions is roughly the same as the percentage of Francophones in our population – and Francophones are above that proportion in lower-paying support jobs and below that proportion at the higher-paying, decision-making, managerial level.

It is of course true that if one wishes to move from the Alberta scene to the national one, to take responsibility for all Canadians, one will have to find the means of communicating with all Canadians. If one is Minister, or Deputy Minister, of Agriculture, one has responsibility for Alberta wheat farmers and cattle ranchers, and also for Quebec dairy farmers and market gardeners. Fishermen speak English in British Columbia, and most speak French in the Gaspé. More jobs in the national capital therefore have to be bilingual. The principle, and this is the wording of the law, is that *federal institutions* have to be able to serve Canadians in our official languages.

What about costs? Annual federal expenditures are over a hundred billion dollars. One per cent of that would be one billion dollars. We spend less than that, about $654,000,000, on Official Languages. $254,000,000 of that is made up of transfer payments from the federal government to the provinces for education. About $335,000,000 goes to services, including language training where needed. That comes to thirteen dollars a year for each of us, about three and a half cents a day. It seems to me that the break-up of our country would be far more costly than that, and far more painful than the irritants some Canadians perceive in our Official Languages system.

Let me say immediately that I take those perceived irritants seriously. I ask your help in identifying them, and in finding solutions for them. I ask you, at the same time, to be sure your facts are right when you criticize the Official Languages Act and its applications. I have no intention of playing games with figures. Let us, together, look facts in the face.

The position of Commissioner of Official Languages has existed since 1970, the year following the adoption of the Official Languages Act. Since the title is too long to fit into a newspaper headline, the Commissioner is sometimes referred to as the "language czar" or "language boss." This is, to put it mildly, a misnomer. The Commissioner has no dictatorial authority; he cannot order anyone to do anything. He makes recommendations, and may find himself making the same recommendation two or three years in a row because it has not been heeded.

He does have a right of judicial recourse, which is to say that in very special cases he can go before the Federal Court on behalf of a complainant and plead for a judgment requiring that some situation be improved. The Commissioner has done so on only two occasions; one case is still pending, and the other was settled out of court. Any citizen, of course, has his or her own right to go before the courts, and the Commissioner may, if he wishes, intervene in such a case in the role of *amicus curiae*, "friend of the court"; he has done so in five instances.

In order to promote proper service to the public, the Commissioner each year does an evaluation of different departments and agencies, and makes such recommendations as may be appropriate.

The Commissioner keeps himself aware of how things are going for our linguistic minorities, and tries to be a bridge between them and the linguistic majorities.

Each person who takes on a responsibility imprints on it something of himself or herself. What is this particular Commissioner of Official Languages trying, hoping to achieve? Above everything else, to help keep Canada together.

Because this is my ultimate, fundamental, over-riding objective, I try to talk, not about constitutions or laws or powers or structures, but about human beings and human relations, about Canadians living together and relating with one another. I want to prevail upon Canadians to feel positively about our country; I seek to motivate English-speaking and French-speaking Canadians to want to keep Canada together.

This country was founded on fairness, and the person who stands before you is deeply committed to fairness and equity in employment and promotion. At the same time, I am responsible for seeing to it that the public is properly served. We cannot serve the Canadian public in one language only. We cannot serve the Canadian public appropriately without designating *some* jobs as bilingual. Because not every federal public servant or applicant to the federal public service is bilingual, the numbers of such jobs should be kept to the minimum necessary for the public, where concentrations of population require it, to be properly served. Fairness requires that each federal public servant have the chance to build a career according to his or her abilities, with language training as required.

Let me point out that there are many jobs which have specific skill requirements: computer language, for example. A high-level career in the Department of National Health and Welfare would be difficult to achieve for a person unfamiliar with health care systems or social welfare problems. What we must ensure is that job skill requirements are realistic and fair; that they represent real needs with regard to serving the public, and that they do not constitute unfair impediments to career advancement.

I want to say to you, as clearly as I possibly can, that I am open to a review of the bilingual designation of any federal public service job, in order to be sure, as objectively as possible, that two-language capability is truly necessary for service to the public. The Commissioner is there to defend the rights of federal public servants as well as those of Canadian citizens in general.

I want to know about the irritants which are felt by many Canadians to be inherent in Official Languages policies and programs. I do not want to sweep them under any rug; I do not want any Canadian to think I am indifferent to them. I want to be told about them, and I want to do something about them. If they are based on misconceptions or on inaccurate information, I want to provide the true facts. If something is not as it should be, is not reasonably necessary for proper service to the public, or constitutes an unfair obstacle to a federal public service career, I want to recommend that it be changed.

There are myths and misapprehensions about what many people call official bilingualism – I prefer to speak of the two-language nature of Canada – and it would be tragic if the country broke apart because of myths and misapprehensions. I want Canada to remain united. I want to reduce the tensions which are making that unity more difficult to preserve. I want Canadians to know the truth about our two-language system.

I am therefore inviting Canadians to write to me. I will respond personally. I would ask only one thing: that each person write on his or her own behalf, write to me about his or her own experience. If you write to me that you know of someone who has had a negative experience with the federal Official Languages program, I cannot investigate it without that person's permission, nor indeed without that person's first-hand account of the facts of the matter. I want to make things better – either to improve the situation itself, if it deserves to be changed, or to improve the feelings of Canadians about Canada as a two-language country.

So I come, in this last part of my address, to historical considerations. Tensions between English-speaking and French-speaking people go a very long way back in the history of the world. A child born today has a reasonable chance of living to experience the one-thousandth anniversary of the Battle of Hastings, the invasion of Britain by Norman France. Many of the heroes of British history are heroes because they defeated the French: Edward III, at Crécy in 1346; Henry V, at Agincourt in 1415; Horatio Nelson, whose statue towers over Trafalgar Square, at Trafalgar in 1805; the Duke of Wellington, at Waterloo in 1815. Joan of Arc is a heroine of France because she defeated the English. It is only in this century, beginning with the First World War, that active friendship has developed between Britain and France.

As those centuries of enmity between French and English unfolded, the conflict eventually affected Canada. In 1534 Jacques Cartier had landed in Gaspé, and in 1535 had sailed up the Saint Lawrence as far as Montreal. French has been part of our heritage ever since. For two and a quarter centuries we were a French domain, and French-speaking people settled here and multiplied.

French-speaking Canadians contributed to the discovery and development of the West. Pierre de la Vérendrye and his sons, in the 1730s and 1740s, extensively explored vast areas from Lake Superior to the Rocky Mountains. Father Lacombe and others contributed significantly to the settlement of the West. Sir Wilfrid Laurier sat for a Saskatchewan riding during his first term as Prime Minister. We have shared a great deal in our history.

It is important. however, to recall that prior to the establishment of French settlement, except for scattered and impermanent colonies of Scandinavian origin, only

the languages of our Aboriginal brothers and sisters were
heard in this land.

It was in the eighteenth century that the war between
France and England broke over Canada. The fortress of
Louisbourg in the south-eastern corner of Cape Breton
Island fell to the British. In 1755 the Acadians were
expelled from Nova Scotia, one of the least glorious
episodes in Canadian history. In 1759, on the Plains
of Abraham outside the walls of Quebec City, Canada
became a British domain.

The victors might easily have decreed that from that
day forward, Canada was a unilingual, English-speaking
country. They did not, and we have been living with two
languages ever since. By the Treaty of Paris in 1763, and
by the Quebec Act of 1774, the French language was
given status in this country. In effect, then, we have had
two official languages for 233 years.

In the past century, and particularly in the past half-
century, the composition of our population has changed
a good deal and become more varied. Many languages
are heard in the land, but only two of them, English and
French, can bind the country together.

That does not mean making the country bilingual from
coast to coast. It does not mean imposing French on
English-speaking Albertans. It does not mean increasing
the numbers of bilingual jobs in this province. It only
means being fair to Canadian citizens.

Yes, there is some degree of compulsion in Quebec. Yes,
Quebec adopted Bill 178, and by so doing engendered a
good deal of resentment in the rest of Canada. The fact
that the provincial domain is outside my jurisdiction has
not prevented me from saying, in Quebec and elsewhere,
that I consider Bill 178 to be wrong and misdirected;
wrong because it is a constraint upon freedom of expression, and misdirected because the security and vitality of
the French language in its minority position within

Canada and within North America will be ensured, not
by the exclusion of English from commercial signs, but
by education, by the ability of French-speaking Canadians
to work in French, and by self-confidence.

In fairness and balance, it must be pointed out that
Quebec has also legislated assurances of the availability and accessibility of health care and social services
in English, and that public funds support the English-
speaking community's three universities, seven colleges
and 350 schools.

I return to a theme of my beginning: we cannot build
a country on bitterness, nor hold it together with anger
and resentment. I want to encourage Canadians, French-
speaking and English-speaking, towards the exercise of
that generosity of spirit which is present in the heart and
mind of almost everyone. I want to be a weaver of understanding, of mutual respect, of a stronger social fabric,
of a better country.

Human nature is made up of elements which cover a
spectrum from positive to negative. If we set out to reinforce negative attitudes, it is dangerously easy to do so.
If, at this critical time in our history, we do not reinforce
the positives which this very special country represents
for us, it may break apart in our hands.

As I said earlier, my thoughts generally formulate themselves in human terms. The person that we know, with
whom we have a relationship, we almost always treat and
consider as a human being. The person that we do not
know, especially if we identify him or her – or the group
to which he or she belongs – as different from ourselves,
whether it be by religion or by culture or by appearance
or by language, all too easily is stereotyped as someone
we dislike. The vast majority of Canadians are likeable,
decent people; let us make that fact the basis for the
unity of our country.

I stand before you as a person who understands some
of the frustrations felt by Western Canadians in their

relation with Central Canada. I stand before you as a person who understands something of the deep, emotional concern of French-speaking Canadians, those in Quebec who have legislative power and those, about a million in number, who live in other parts of Canada and essentially do not, that their language may in the long run be in danger.

I stand before you as a Canadian convinced that if this country breaks up, the resulting fragments will each be weaker in economic strength, less significant in trade relationships, less influential in international affairs and less secure than the united country we have today.

My grandparents, all four of them, came to Canada from eastern Europe a little over a century ago. Montreal was their port of entry, but my father's parents lived most of their lives in Vancouver. My grandparents came in search of freedom from persecution, of equal opportunity, of decency and fairness. They gave me, through their profound gratitude for those things, my love of this country and my commitment to it.

I look around the world today, and I see people fighting each other and pulling apart from one another because of religious or linguistic or ethnic or cultural differences, and I thank God for Canada. I thank God for a country in which Canadians of Jewish heritage and Canadians of Arab heritage can talk to one another, and Irish Protestant Canadians and Irish Catholic Canadians can talk to one another, and I hope that Canadians with Serbian roots and Canadians with Croatian roots are able to talk with one another – and I want to maintain a Canada in which English-speaking Canadians and French-speaking Canadians can manage to talk with one another. This last is in one respect more difficult, because two languages are involved.

That is where I, as Commissioner of Official Languages, come in.

Precisely because I do not wish to force any Canadian to be bilingual who does not wish to be so, I want to be a communications agent, a builder of bridges, a promoter of understanding, a purveyor of truth. I want to prevail on you to share my positive vision of this country's past, present and future.

# Quebec

In my younger days it was common – and accurate – to say that if a committee was composed of five francophones and one anglophone, everyone had to speak English because the anglophone could neither speak nor understand French. (And it was considered normal, although resented, that the anglophone should receive that deference.) Today the exact opposite is widely true, but the subconscious memory of that imbalance has not entirely faded.

In the course of the twentieth century, English came to dominate the world and to be the lingua franca of international communication. At less than 2 per cent of the total population of North America, French-speaking Canadians have long felt apprehensive about the survival of their language and culture. Quebec, as it emerged into the bright light of the Quiet Revolution, came to feel politically able to do something about it.

Freedom of choice is a fundamental principle of democracy, and it presented Quebec with a particularly difficult challenge. As the birth rate fell dramatically in the 1960s and immigration became the only source of population growth, allophone families gravitated massively to English-language schools. Although a profoundly and genuinely democratic society in every other respect, Quebec developed a determination to stem that tide. In 1969 the Union nationale government of Jean-Jacques Bertrand brought in Bill 63. Its potential impact was minimal, and the Liberal opposition supported it, but a rump of five MNAs from both sides of the house mounted a vocal opposition, and so Bill 63's only real effect was to provide a small early impetus to the sovereignist movement.

Robert Bourassa came to power in 1970 and was re-elected with a large majority in 1973. In neither election campaign did he make any mention of language legislation, but in 1974 he brought in Bill 22, which made French the official language of Quebec and placed limits on access to English-language schools. The English-speaking community reacted with fierce and almost universal anger. Robert, who did not know the English-speaking community very well, except for the business sector, was undoubtedly taken by surprise by the intensity of the reaction. He tolerated loud condemnation from his rank-and-file anglophone MNAs, but his three English-speaking ministers – William Tetley of Notre-Dame-de-Grâce, Kevin Drummond of Westmount (who subsequently became a Péquiste), and I – were bound by cabinet solidarity and could not speak out. There were widespread calls for our resignation.

Cabinet solidarity is basic to the parliamentary system that Canada inherited from Britain. Issues are thrashed out at the cabinet table – I was forthright in my opposition to Bill 22 and explicit in communicating the anger of the English-speaking community – but once a decision is taken, no minister can speak or vote against it.

In the 1976 election campaign the anger, which had faded somewhat, boiled over again. I kept pointing out that of the 800,000 anglophones in Quebec, 799,997 had been free to speak out – and did – and three were not. In the D'Arcy McGee riding the Union nationale, which in 1973 had received 700 votes, got 7,000 with a virtually unknown candidate. I was re-elected, but the Parti Québécois became the government.

By comparison with what came after, Bill 22 was relatively mild. It allowed English-speaking children into English-language schools, but blocked immigrants if they were not fluent in English. It essentially pleased no one – in good measure because it was bad legislation. The worst thing about it was its method for determining admissibility to English-language schooling. Instead of interviewing the family, the assessors tested the six-year-old child, unaccompanied and possibly terrified. The resentment this approach engendered was understandably deep.

There was more – and I pointed this out to Robert Bourassa and to my good friend François Cloutier, who was the minister legislatively responsible for the bill. François understood; Robert did not. When you test a group of children, presumably some will pass and some will not. Those who pass will be rewarded. Those who fail will be penalized. The prize was going to an English-language school. The penalty was going to a French-language school. This was a strange message. Also, the ones who pass are likely to be the brightest, and *they* were going to be selected for English-language schooling.

Bill 22 pleased virtually no one, and it was of no benefit to Robert Bourassa in the 1976 election. The Parti Québécois judged it inadequate and brought in Bill 101, which came to be called the Charter of the French Language. English-speaking anger was just as intense as with Bill 22, but there was no English-speaking presence in the PQ cabinet, and there were no established lines of communication with the new government. Bill 101 passed, with the Liberals voting against it, and Quebec, irreversibly, entered a new era.

Many anglophones, especially the young and mobile, moved out of the province. Others assessed the situation and set about devising means of coping with it. Within days of the passage of Bill 101, a group of young professionals came together and created Participation Quebec. Committed to active involvement in Quebec society, they looked analytically at the new context and assessed how to adapt to it and how to contest some of the difficulties it posed. Soon afterwards, Alex Paterson and Storrs McCall established the Positive Action Committee, which brought together significant elements of English-speaking community leadership. A subsequent creation was the Council of Quebec Minorities. In 1981 a decision was made to establish a province-wide community organization, and in 1982 Alliance Quebec's founding convention took place.

Eric Maldoff was chosen president. My son Michael was vice-president and subsequently became A Q's second president. Intelligent strategy was the watchword. Lines of communication were opened with the Parti Québécois government, with English-language institutions, with English-language minority communities all over the province, with the media, and with public opinion. Alliance Quebec, recognizing that in a win-lose situation the English-speaking community was not often likely to win, went into action when it felt that something fundamental was at stake, and on other issues it sought a middle-ground accommodation.

In structural terms, there had never been an English-speaking community before. Alliance Quebec linked hospitals and school boards and municipalities and universities and social service organizations (setting aside their long-standing religious identifications), and it reached out to grassroots citizens. It also linked the Townshippers, C A S A (Committee for Anglophone Social Action) in the Gaspé, the Coasters on the Far North Shore, the Voice of English Quebec in Quebec City, the Outaouais Alliance, and more, into a relatively cohesive association. It channelled energies into a coordinated strategy.

Alliance Quebec had two basic objectives: to help the English-speaking community evolve in its ability to live with the new reality and to protect English-language institutions. The predominance of French in Quebec was clearly irreversible; the sustained vitality of the English-speaking community could not be taken for granted and required a vigorous defence. Successes, in negotiations with an ideologically motivated government, were not easy to come by. Battles had to be chosen wisely. One notable achievement was shifting the responsibility of providing service in French in public institutions from the shoulders of each individual to those of the institution. Today patients are looked after in French in every English-speaking hospital.

There were successes. René Lévesque and Gérald Godin among his ministers were people of dialogue, and Eric Maldoff negotiated a bill that eased a few of the restrictions in Bill 101. A little later Michael, dealing now with a Liberal government, obtained the introduction of Bill 142, which ensured access to health care and social services in English. It recognized that language is an instrument of treatment. Since success was sometimes elusive, however, it was easy to be critical. Diplomacy was decried by some vocal people, who called Alliance Quebec the "lamb lobby." Ultimately, the hard-liners took over, and AQ was run into the ground. Somewhat later the vacuum was filled by the Quebec Community Groups Network. The QCGN gave us the signal honour of creating the Sheila and Victor Goldbloom Award for community service.

Alliance Quebec was vilified by many in the French-speaking community as well – and even, thoughtlessly, by Robert Bourassa, who said, "I am caught between two extremisms, the Société Saint-Jean-Baptiste and Alliance Quebec." It was his use of the notwithstanding clause to negate a Supreme Court of Canada decision which undermined Alliance Quebec and put wind in the sails of the anglophone hard line. It also probably contributed to the defeat of the Meech Lake Accord.

The English-speaking community has made enormous progress in the ninety years of my involvement in it. Today French is spoken effectively and comfortably by a large majority of anglophones. English-French communication is much more generalized and natural. Bill 101 is part of the landscape, and most anglophones, although they wish it was not there, would rather live with it than with more radical measures that are proposed from time to time.

Unfortunately, this extraordinary evolution of the English-speaking community is largely unrecognized among the French-speaking majority. Because the English language is seen as the competitive danger, the English-speaking community is still perceived by many – some political leaders among them – unfairly and inaccurately, as the enemy. Although almost all French-speaking parents, whatever their political persuasion, want their children to learn English, public policy remains repressive, and some groups want it to be made even more so. The English-speaking community is deeply committed to Quebec, deeply sensitive to the existential concerns of its French-speaking fellow citizens, and deeply desirous of moving forward together.

That community has, however, suffered significant losses since 1976. Young people, always more mobile, have in appreciable numbers sought their future elsewhere. School enrolments have fallen, partly because of a low birth rate but also because of legislation restricting access. The community has had greater difficulty in maintaining its institutions. It has paid, in my view, a much heavier price than was necessary.

It is my conviction that French will not survive primarily through legislation. The pride that parents and teachers, and public officials, and people in general feel in their language, heritage, and way of life is the ultimate determining factor. As a bridge-builder across the linguistic divide, I have been privileged to share and to foster that pride, and to help protect the English-speaking community at the same time.

Bill 101, widely regarded among the French-speaking majority as sacred and virtually untouchable, has been and is still – although to a lesser degree today – a stressful experience for the English-speaking minority. It is worth observing, however, that since the preservation of the French language has been the most fundamental objective of the separatist movement, the linguistic protection afforded by Bill 101 has almost certainly diminished the motivation for political autonomy.

## REASONABLE ACCOMMODATION

In the last third of the twentieth century, Quebec's persistently low birth rate caused governments to focus on immigration. With the influx of people from various parts of the world, religions that had been tiny minorities became significant components of Quebec society. From time to time, strictly practising members of such religions would request special arrangements to accommodate their pattern of worship: a place to pray, a day off without penalty for a religious holiday, a separation of facilities for men and women.

Most such situations were worked out by mutual agreement, but occasionally one would make headlines. The government decided to create a commission to study the issue and named Gérard Bouchard and Charles Taylor as its members. Before beginning public hearings throughout the province in 2007, Bouchard and Taylor held a series of preliminary conversations with selected groups. The Jewish community was one of them. Bouchard put the question "Why here? And why now?" I answered that it was here because of the ongoing existential anxiety of French-speaking Quebecers, and it was now because certain immigrant groups were perceived as resistant to integration into Quebec society.

The commission's hearings included open-microphone sessions allowing any individual to express his or her views, and not a few took advantage of the opportunity to vent attitudes that were sometimes quite racist. It was felt by many, myself included, that the commissioners were over-tolerant of such nastiness and did not react to it promptly enough; but generally Quebec came across as a thoughtful and generous society that simply did not want to have its way of life altered.

The Quebec Jewish Congress appeared towards the end of the process. I was accompanied by Dorothy Zalcman Howard and Jo Gabay. Our brief was descriptive of our community and our religion, and we spelled out our position on the key issues. I quoted the dictum of the third-century sage Samuel of Babylon: "Dinah d'malchutah dinah" (the law of the land is the law). We took the position that the wearing of religious symbols or clothing should be a personal matter. We pointed out that the integration of adult immigrants may present certain difficulties, but that the integration of their children, educated and socialized in our schools, would be far less problematic. And we said that the majority has rights, notably the right to continuity and to the maintenance of its traditions and values.

Following the hearings, I took our brief on the road. Through the good offices of Guy Bouthillier, a friend who was a past president of the Société Saint-Jean-Baptiste de Montréal, and those of QJC executive director Daniel Amar, I was able to obtain speaking engagements with nine SSJBs (now called Mouvement national des Québécois) in different parts of the province. It had been my conclusion that whereas antisemitism in Quebec had not vanished, it was now a marginal phenomenon, and that our major problem was that our community was essentially unknown – and in the current context, perceived as one among many immigrant incursions.

In places such as Saint-Jean-sur-Richelieu, Drummondville, Mont-Laurier, Valleyfield, and Trois-Rivières, I spoke about our two and a half centuries of history in Quebec, our integration – except for our 12–13 per cent of ultra-Orthodox – and our signal contributions to Quebec society. I was received cordially and attentively, and rewarded each time by the same two reactions: "You have corrected a lot of false impressions I had about your community" and "Hey, you're Quebecers just like us."

Prior to the Quiet Revolution, religion – one religion – had dominated Quebec society. Diversity was not a conspicuous feature of that society, and no need was felt for public policy in majority-minority relations. As religious practice decreased within the majority population, the intensity of observance among, for example, Sikhs or Muslims or ultra-Orthodox Jews came to be perceived as a threatening challenge. With the low birth rate remaining stagnant, the prospect of continuing immigration fostered anxiety about the future of the French language and about Quebec's way of life. Although most places of worship had fewer congregants than before, religion remained important in the lives of considerable numbers of people, and there was reaction, of which I was supportive, against its marginalization.

Quebec sought to benefit from the experiences of other countries, notably of France, but also to define its own home-grown policies. Canada's forty-year-old multiculturalism had come to have negative resonance in Quebec, which saw it as intensifying threats against the province's culture. The majority felt that they were being required to accommodate to other religions, rather than the immigrants being obliged to adapt to Quebec society and integrate into it. In 2013 the Parti Québécois, in power but with a minority of seats in the legislature, decided to respond by putting forward a bill that was alternatively called the Charter of Secularization or the Charter of Quebec Values. It proposed that the wearing of conspicuous religious symbols or clothing be banned in the public service, and it extended this restriction to publicly funded institutions such as hospitals, schools, and universities. Everyone knew, and some said openly, that the target group was Muslim women who wore the hijab or other veiling garments. The turbans of Sikh men and kippot (skullcaps) of Orthodox Jews were, however, also to be illegal in public institutions.

Negative reaction was widespread, but it was not limited to those communities. Within the French-speaking majority, many people spoke out against the bill, including Gérard Bouchard, Charles Taylor, former Parti Québécois premiers Jacques Parizeau, Lucien Bouchard, and Bernard Landry, and former Bloc Québécois leader Gilles Duceppe. The Quebec Human Rights Commission and the Quebec Bar were clear in their opposition. The government ignored them all.

Public hearings were convened before a parliamentary committee, and the Christian-Jewish Dialogue of Montreal, of which I was the chairperson, submitted a brief. My colleagues Diane Rollert, a minister of the Unitarian Church, and Jean Duhaime, the retired dean of Religious Studies at the Université de Montréal, worked with me on the text. We went beyond the religious symbols issue and focused on the broader effect of the law in silencing religions and making them invisible. We recognized that religions have some negative things in their records, but some very positive ones as well, and that although religious practice is somewhat less widespread than it used to be, it is still important in the lives of a great many Quebec citizens. We urged that the government limit itself to declaring the state to be religiously neutral, and that it drop the juridical complexities which would, in our view (but not in the government's), make a court challenge inevitable and successful.

There were two questions that gave me the opportunity of emphatic responses. (Both came from the opposition side of the table.) One was about the government's assertion that it was harmful for a young child to be exposed to a diversity of religious symbols. I was asked my opinion as a pediatrician, and I said that the most fundamental right that a schoolchild has is to be prepared to face the world, and that it makes no sense to hide from him or her, in the classroom, the reality of religious diversity which is there just outside the door of the school.

The other question concerned discrimination, and I answered that I had grown up in a Quebec which had discriminatory barriers and selectively limited opportunities; that until I arrived in 1970, there had never been a Jewish member of the Quebec cabinet; and that therefore I was allergic to any distinction between human beings which was based on religious affiliation.

## QUEBEC AND CANADA

Of all the tasks of bridge-building I have faced, that between Quebec and Canada, between federalists and sovereignists,

has been the most challenging. It is a fundamental principle
in dialogue that one must not only listen to the other person's
positions and perceptions, but one must strive to achieve a
sense of how that person feels in his or her skin, to walk a kilo-
metre in his or her shoes.

My federalism has been unshakeable – I worked hard for the
"No" side in the 1980 referendum – but I am not dismissive of
the concerns of my sovereignist friends. I understand intellectually their desire for an autonomous country – early Péquistes
would express admiration for the State of Israel, which had
achieved independence *and* had preserved a language – but I
have the conviction that my friends underestimate the difficulties of negotiations with the rest of Canada and the complexities and costs with which a new country would have to cope.
And I think that Canada, although it has difficulties in its ongoing relations with Quebec, is committed to French, to being
the second most important country in the Francophonie, and
to making Quebec prosper and succeed – and even to recognizing, respecting, and supporting its distinctiveness.

Obviously, the desire to have Quebec separate from Canada
is based on the perception that the province has been hampered in its development and in its ability to protect its language and culture. I have been a Quebec minister and have
opposed some federal policies and programs, but on balance
I feel that Quebec has prospered within the federation and
that Canada has supported French and is committed to the
country's voice being heard in both languages.

As Commissioner of Official Languages, I saw French-
speaking Canada as a whole. I got to know the French-
speaking minorities in every province and territory, some of
which have impressive vitality, and I have enormous respect
for *their* determination to preserve their language, transmit it
to their children, maintain their historic traditions, and live
in French. I wanted Quebec, a major potential resource close
at hand, to be supportive of them, but that appeal had virtually no resonance; for sovereignists, only Quebec could preserve French in North America.

In the early days of Péquiste governance, although René Lévesque, Jacques-Yvan Morin, Robert Burns, and a few others were open to conversation, hostility was much more prevalent on both sides. It took time before a normal level of parliamentary adversarial discourse and of human relations returned, but it did. I strove to be part of the bridge-building, and when I made my farewell speech in the National Assembly, virtually all the Péquiste ministers and MNAs came over to express their regard.

I received a generous compliment from Richard Guay, who had been a Parti Québécois minister and a distinguished speaker of the National Assembly. We had subsequently, in political retirement, worked together on a task force charged with reviewing MNAs' pensions. He came to speak at McGill University, and recognizing my presence in the audience, he commented that there are relatively few parliamentarians who become respected on both sides of the house and that I was one of that number.

I have been privileged to be in continuing demand on French-language radio and television, as well as in English and to some degree in the print media as well. My public discourse has been fairly widely heard. I have been made to feel a part of Quebec society in a way that I could not have imagined when I was young. I am touched by the relations of mutual respect that I have had, and have, with people of different political persuasions.

One of the most moving encounters I have ever had occurred one day when I emerged onto University Street from the side door of the Royal Victoria Hospital. I had found a parking spot right there, and as I approached my car a gentleman, a stranger, was unlocking the door of his in front of mine. He put his key back in his pocket and came over to me, shook my hand, and said, "If there were more federalists like you, there would be fewer separatists like me." And he walked away.

# "Retirement," 1999–

My favourite lines of poetry are from Tennyson's "Ulysses":

How dull it is to pause, to make an end,
To rust unburnish'd, not to shine in use!
As tho' to breathe were life.

I left the commissioner's office without any future plans, except for an imprecise intention to continue in interreligious relations and a strong resistance to the notion of permanent vacation. Reading, crossword puzzles, and Sudoku were intellectually stimulating, as of course were theatre, concerts, and art exhibitions. Grandchildren were a joy, but they had their own lives. Carrying responsibility, thinking through public issues, was what life was about.

Three anxious days went by before the phone rang and someone asked me to do something – and it has not stopped since. I had continued to attend, when I could, the meetings of the Christian-Jewish Dialogue of Montreal and those of the Canadian Christian-Jewish Consultation. The Canadian Jewish Congress welcomed me back to an active role, and other opportunities, notably in the health care field, began to arise. My days were full again.

Christian-Jewish dialogue was a half-century old and had considerably evolved. The positive impact of *Nostra Aetate* and the Second Vatican Council was undimmed, and there was sustained motivation for moving steadily forward. Conscious of the fact that dialogue would not change society if it remained limited to a dozen or so people sitting around a table, enjoying each other's company and finding reward in the conversation, we put together conferences from time to time and welcomed new partners into the circle. As a past president of the International Council of Christians and Jews (ICCJ), I continued to attend its annual colloquia and ensured that Canada's chair was occupied at the annual general meetings. And I was appointed to the Interreligious Relations Committee of the Union for Reform Judaism, headquartered in Washington, DC. I was the only Canadian.

Dialogue took on new dimensions as new partners joined. The Ukrainian community arrived at the Christian-Jewish Dialogue of Montreal (CJDM), to a warm welcome. After a while, we created a bilateral Ukrainian-Jewish dialogue, as an offshoot from the main table. It has flourished ever since. A later arrival was the Church of Jesus Christ of Latter-Day Saints, the Mormon Church, with similar success.

Relations between the Jewish and Christian communities and the Muslim community were a growing concern in the face of world and even local events. There had been a Jewish-Muslim dialogue in English for a decade or so, and the opportunity arose to establish one in French. I met Touhami Rachid Raffa, originally from Algeria, we struck it off well, and the hoped-for dialogue began. It carried on successfully for some time, but some key participants were transferred away and it petered out – hopefully to be revived in a not too distant future.

There were new initiatives at the national level as well, led notably by the Reverend Karen Hamilton, general secretary of the Canadian Council of Churches (CCC), a past chairperson of the Canadian Christian-Jewish Consultation (CCJC). When the G8 and G20 met in Canada in 2009, she brought together a multi-religious group to present a joint statement to the government leaders. That led to cooperation regarding a national anti-poverty strategy in Canada and a responsible approach to climate change, and I was very much involved in these latter undertakings.

Karen is an exemplar of the quality of leadership that dialogue has had. I am greatly indebted to her, as I am to many people. I select only a few names: the late Rabbi Harry Joshua Stern, Rabbi Howard Joseph, Rabbi Leigh Lerner, and Archbishop Marcel Gervais of Ottawa, a stalwart support. At the international level, I have had special esteem for Dr Gerhart Riegner, the general secretary of the World Jewish Congress; for Eugene Fisher, senior staff person for the US Conference of Catholic Bishops; and for Father John Pawlikowski of Chicago. I deeply miss Rabbi Michael Signer, who taught at Notre Dame University in the United States and was a principal author of the important document *Dabru Emet* (speak the truth), a sensitive Jewish reflection on Christianity.

In 2012 a crisis arose in Christian-Jewish relations. In August of that year the United Church of Canada held its triennial General Council and adopted a boycott of products originating in Israel's West Bank settlements. I was invited to address the delegates. I received a genuinely warm welcome from them on an individual basis, but I was amazed at how uninformed these decent and well-meaning people were about the Middle East. My brief, time-limited intervention was preceded by the three authors of the resolution, one of whom was downright nasty, and followed by a Palestinian gentleman who was cordial as an individual but left a thoroughly negative message. The debate was engineered in such a way as to convey the assumption that the motion would pass – which it did. I walked out. The Jewish community reacted .to the one-sidedness and one-track-mindedness of this decision and suspended its participation in the national dialogue table, the Canadian Christian-Jewish Consultation, though dialogue was maintained at the local level in Montreal, Toronto, and other cities.

Earlier in my career, full-time pediatric practice had prevented me from taking on community involvement, but from
my entry into public life in 1966 I had been very attentive to
the Canadian Jewish Congress. In retirement, I gravitated to it
and ultimately became president of Quebec Region and
chairperson of the national executive. Congress was an intelligent organization that was immediately responsive, nation-
ally and locally, to issues arising in Canadian society. It dealt
strategically with those regarding the Jewish community and
had a sensitive social conscience with respect to those of concern to the whole of society.

There is a deeply held Jewish tradition of the responsibility
of human beings for one another and of a community for its
members in difficulty. Quebec's Jewish community has 18–20
per cent of its members living below the poverty line, and it
raises funds each year accordingly. It also has over 20 per cent
of senior citizens, twice the Quebec average, and must cope
with their needs. It is, per capita, the most generous Jewish
community in all of North America.

In 2008 a decision was made by a group of influential men
to restructure the community and do away with Congress,
notwithstanding its distinguished ninety-year record of accom-
plishment. I worked constructively with the new organization,
but it was not the same. It is called the Centre for Israel and
Jewish Affairs (CIJA) – no mention of Canada – and it has
diminished the community's historic preoccupation with social
issues. Its primary focus is Israel. I am a supporter and
defender of Israel, but I am also a concerned Canadian with
an intense interest in quality-of-life matters: those affecting
my community and those affecting our society as a whole.

During my tenure as president of Quebec Region, I had felt
increasingly that that was not an appropriate name. I thought
we needed to make it clear that the Jewish community was an
integral and contributing part of Quebec society. We adopted
the name "Quebec Jewish Congress, a division of Canadian
Jewish Congress," and this change had a positive impact on
majority public opinion.

The Jewish community, having been directed by legislation in the early twentieth century into the Protestant school system, was almost entirely English-speaking until after World War II. Postwar immigration brought small numbers of francophones, for example, from Romania, where French was traditionally the second language of educated people. In the 1960s a substantial flow of Sephardic immigration from Morocco changed the community's linguistic composition and its religious traditions. Sephardim now constitute over 20 per cent of the community.

The language barrier made the English-speaking Ashkenazic majority less welcoming than it ought to have been. As one of the rare Ashkenazic French-speakers, I reached out to both of these groups and became involved in the organizations they created. It took some years before the Sephardic component produced community leaders, but when Jo Gabay became president of the Quebec Jewish Congress and Sylvain Abitbol president of Federation-CJA and later co-president of the Canadian Jewish Congress, the bridge had been built.

The Sephardic community became the Canadian component of the Alliance Israélite Universelle, a century-old organization with schools in various parts of the world. One of its leading figures for many years was the French jurist and Nobel Prize–winner René Cassin, one of the authors, as was John P. Humphrey of Canada, of the Universal Declaration of Human Rights. I met him on two occasions when he visited Montreal, and I was deeply honoured when the AIU presented me with its René Cassin Medal.

In 1969, when I was an opposition MNA, I had asked to see Premier Jean-Jacques Bertrand, who had been education minister before he became premier. The issue was the discrimination against Jewish parents with children in the Protestant school system: they paid their school taxes into the system, but were not entitled to vote in school board elections and could not run for the position of commissioner. (This prejudice was finally abolished in 1972 under Education Minister Guy Saint-Pierre.)

Premier Bertrand, for whom I had a high regard, received me with his characteristic gentlemanly cordiality. Open on his desk in front of him was one of the thick volumes of the *Statuts refondus du Québec*, the compendium of Quebec laws. He put his finger on the article of the "Loi sur l'instruction publique" that read, "For the purposes of education, Jewish children shall be considered to be Protestants," and he turned to me and said, "This is one of the worst mistakes ever made by a Quebec legislature."

I had been asked in 1999 to join the board and executive of my synagogue, Temple Emanu-El–Beth Sholom, and in 2000 I was elected president. The term is limited to two years in the bylaws, but for a third and a fourth year a resolution was passed to waive that restriction and allow me to continue. In 2012 Rabbi Leigh Lerner unexpectedly announced his retirement. He had served the congregation, to widespread admiration throughout the community, for twenty-three years. I had been on the search committee which chose him, and I was named to chair the team to find his successor. We worked diligently and harmoniously, considered fourteen candidacies, shortened the list to six and then to four, and chose Rabbi Lisa Grushcow, an Ottawa native, a McGill graduate, and a Rhodes Scholar, as the first female senior rabbi in the history of Montreal. Simply put, we chose well. She quickly became an intellectual leader in the community and in the wider world and a thoughtful contributor to the debate on the role of religion in an increasingly secular society.

Temple Emanu-El–Beth Sholom is the only Reform synagogue in Montreal, a community that is less inclined towards Reform Judaism than most of North America. I had been brought up in a relatively Orthodox congregation, Shaar Hashomayim, and came to Temple when our daughter, Susan, was born and Sheila and I wanted our family to be able to sit together. It has been a top-notch intellectual experience, both in terms of the understanding it has cultivated of our

religion and because of the cultural programming it has
always maintained. Reform ("progressive" or "liberal") Judaism
is less rigid about religious restrictions and has long maintained gender equality. It has become the dominant movement in the United States, although not yet in Canada.

As the twenty-first century began, the demographics of the
Jewish community were becoming a concern. The birth rate,
like that of Quebec as a whole, was about 1.4, far below
replacement level, and as noted earlier, over 20 per cent of
members were senior citizens. It became clear that immigration was the only means of stemming further shrinkage. I was
named to head a task force to design and implement a strategy in this regard.

A severe economic crisis had struck Argentina. The largely
middle-class Jewish community had been particularly hard
hit. Unsure of whether that community would want to struggle through or would encourage its young people to seek a
better future elsewhere, I made two trips to Buenos Aires and
diplomatically tested the waters. We were not perceived as
predators, and hundreds of young families came to put down
new roots in Montreal.

France was experiencing a troubling rise in antisemitism,
some of it violent. Emigration is not well regarded by the
French, but Quebec is still perceived as an important part of
the French-speaking world, and moving here is not seen quite
as negatively. I took similar diplomatic initiatives in Paris, with
considerable help from the Quebec government, and significant numbers of young people came to join our community.

Although I was no longer practising pediatrics, I continued to
be actively interested in the functioning of the health care
system. For a decade I chaired the Jewish Public Establishments
Coordinating Committee, which met regularly to consider
policy issues and practical matters concerning the community's health care and social service institutions, and to pursue

government relations, which I led. I negotiated, with the excellent health minister Pierre Marc Johnson, the move of Mount Sinai Hospital from Préfontaine in the Laurentians to a new facility in Montreal. Eventually I was elected to the board of the Agence de la santé et des services sociaux de Montréal.

This body (which had not always had its present name) managed the health care system on the Island of Montreal. Originally its members were elected to represent different components of Quebec society, but a few years ago the government decided to appoint everyone. I had served on this board for three years in the 1980s, and I returned to it after my retirement as Commissioner of Official Languages. Kathleen Weil was president, an articulate spokesperson and an effective leader. One day, out of a clear blue sky, she called me to say that she was resigning (as we learned, to become executive director of the Fondation du Grand Montréal) and would put my name forward to succeed her. My colleagues did me the honour of re-electing me for over a decade afterwards.

Through all the years of my involvement, the Agence had been impressively competent and even-handed, dealing objectively and equitably with the English-speaking and French-speaking institutions and with those of minority communities such as mine. It had a conspicuous social conscience and had produced, notably through its Public Health department, a number of top-notch studies on social determinants of health. As board chairman of the Agence, I had for several years represented the health sector on the Forum des partenaires of the Conférence régionale des élus de Montréal (CRÉ). I incarnated the Agence's social conscience by presenting those reports to my colleagues representing the various key sectors of society.

In 2014 the Quebec government brought forward legislation abolishing the *agences*. I personally thought that this was an error, that it would make the administration of the health care system more remote from and less responsive to the public we serve. It seemed inevitable that our *agence's* tradition of a monthly hour of questions from the public and answers from our chief executive officer would fall by the wayside. I deeply regretted the proposal to amalgamate eight or ten institutions in each area into one, particularly since doing so would eliminate some 90 per cent of the dedicated community volunteers serving on their boards. I was concerned at the possible loss of the ethnic or religious specificity of particular community institutions. The Minister of Health gave assurances that rights to health care and social services in English would be maintained, but I was unconvinced that this commitment would provide permanent protection against a later decision by a less sympathetic government. It seemed to me that an English-speaking community of this size should not be considered to have rights only if it represented at least 51 per cent of the clientele or the staff of a given entity.

The Canadian Institute of Child Health is an Ottawa-based organization that advocates for children. I chair its advisory council. Major preoccupations have been the health effects of various environmental exposures, the particular impacts of such exposures on the unborn child, the socio-economic determinants of health, and the disadvantaged health status of Aboriginal Canadian children. Every few years the CICH publishes a "Profile of the Health of Canada's Children," and it calls public and governmental attention to issues regarding children's health and safety.

In Montreal the Queen Elizabeth Hospital had been a valued community resource for a great many years. When the Quebec government decided to close it, along with the Herbert Reddy and five other hospitals, three of them in the French-speaking community, there was a significant grass-roots reaction. It was stronger in the case of the QEH than for any other institution, because of the human and professional quality of the care it had provided and also because of its location in eastern Notre-Dame-de-Grâce. The alternative resources, St Mary's and the Jewish General, were on the other side of the mountain, and reaching them by public transport is complicated.

As it became evident that the decision was irreversible, the idea of transforming the QEH into an ambulatory health centre began to take shape. It was clear that we could not get a permit for a hospital, but it was also evident that a wide range of services could be offered to the local community. Sheila and I were approached to co-chair the necessary fundraising campaign, and we signed on.

The community support came through, and the Queen Elizabeth Health Complex was created. I was convinced that the McGill University Health Centre, just down the street at the Glen, would have to concentrate on complex cases and would need an ancillary front-line resource. I entered into discussions with the MUHC, and as a result, McGill's Family Medicine unit took space in the QEHC and began to operate our walk-in clinic. The QEHC was an immediate success. The community responded generously, and good people joined the board. A second fundraising campaign made possible the digitization of the x-ray department, and the available rental spaces were progressively filled. The substantial community clientele confirmed the value of the initiative.

In 2003 I was asked to serve on the Quebec government's jury for awards for bravery. Recommendations are received, largely from the general public, and each is bolstered by attestations from witnesses and from appropriate authorities (police, fire, and others). An experienced professional checks out each one, and the jury devotes a full day to evaluating thirty or forty dossiers. A point scale is used – what was the degree of difficulty? to what extent did the rescuer put his or her life in danger? and so on – and the candidate may receive a medal, a certificate of honourable mention, or a letter of commendation from the minister. A ceremony is held in the Red Chamber of the National Assembly, and the Minister of Justice presents the awards.

It is striking, year after year, that the individuals who have unselfishly and spontaneously carried out these dangerous feats – pulling a person from a burning building or from a wrecked car or truck, saving a person from drowning – are in majority not muscular and heroic-looking. Sometimes a child is decorated. It is a moving ceremony, and I have been privileged to be a part of it.

Some years ago, it was decided to create an association of former members of the National Assembly, which was named L'Amicale des anciens parlementaires du Québec. People of all parties come together once a year for a business meeting and a program that generally has a historical context. It is a recognition of the fact that democracy requires adversaries, but that policy disagreements do not prevent mutual respect. The Amicale has created two awards, the Prix Jean-Noël Lavoie for service to the association and the Prix René-Chaloult for overall career accomplishments. I was deeply touched to receive the latter in 2012.

I owe a great debt to my alma mater, McGill University – not only for the degrees I earned and for the many things I was able to accomplish as a student, but also for the sustained relationships I have had over all these years: with successive principals and chancellors, with ICAN, with the opera program, with the McGill Symphony Orchestra, with the libraries, with the Faculty of Religious Studies, notably under the deeply regretted Dean Ellen Aitken, with the McGill Institute for the Study of Canada, and many more. McGill bestowed on me an honorary degree – as did Toronto, Concordia, Ottawa, and Sainte-Anne in Nova Scotia – and very specially, McGill chose me, together with astronaut Julie Payette and extraordinary pianist Oliver Jones, to be the honorary chairpersons of its 175th anniversary.

# Looking Forward

A memoir is by definition a look backwards, and after nine-tenths of a century, one has more to recall than to anticipate. I would like, however, to look forward, to record my hopes, before I close.

## Gender Equality

I learned about gender equality by marrying Sheila. Her professional development was as important as mine, and so were her career and her community involvements and the rewards and recognitions she received. I took for granted, and ensured, that our daughter, Susan, would have the same educational and career opportunities as sons Michael and Jonathan. Such equality was inconceivable to my grandparents, and it was not achieved by my parents' generation.

As president of the International Council of Christians and Jews, I was responsible for the creation of the Women's Council, which existed for many years under the leadership of Gunnel Borgegård of Sweden. Often, then and afterwards, I was virtually the council's only male supporter, but in each country where we held our annual conference, our women reached out to women who were confined to a secondary role within their religion or their society and gave them hope, encouragement, and guidance. And as a physician working on the structure and functioning of our health care system, I made a point of communicating with nurses' organizations and envisioning a more significant professional role for nurses in making the system more effective and more responsive in patient care.

One of my most rewarding experiences was to chair the search committee that chose Lisa Grushcow as senior rabbi of Temple Emanu-El–Beth Sholom. The committee, because several women I had approached had declined, ended up being seven men and three women. Lisa was our overwhelming choice. One of her colleagues at Rodeph Sholom in New York, the synagogue she had served as assistant rabbi for nine very successful years, congratulated us on ensuring that Lisa would "shatter the glass ceiling."

Danielle McCann's arrival as head of the Montreal Health and Social Services Agency caused me to reflect once again on the professional competence of today's women, a competence that was kept latent for so much of human history. She was succeeded by Patricia Gauthier. It is my hope that gender equality, not yet totally achieved, will become the irreversible reality it needs to be.

Still today, in many countries all over the world, women are handicapped by gender discrimination. It is inconceivable that any nation can be a success while repressing 50 per cent of its population. We have learned that, in international aid, microfinancing of women allows them to launch enterprises and support their families, that the repayment of these loans is close to universal, and that women use such funds more responsibly than men.

Canada is a country of opportunity, but it still has something of a glass ceiling. We need to continue working on gender equality, to ensure that women have equality of opportunity for education, equality of consideration for management positions, and equality of remuneration.

## The Health Care System

Canada has a good health care system, but it is not good enough. Our outcomes fall short of those in the Scandinavian countries and the Netherlands – in infant mortality, for example – and we do not respond to patients' needs nearly as promptly or as sensitively as in countries like France. We need to ensure that every citizen has timely access to front-line care and to specialized skill when needed. As well, each person or family should be in the charge of a health care manager, a traffic director who will ensure that tests and consultations are obtained with minimal delay, that test results are promptly recorded and communicated, and that follow-up is attentively sustained. That manager may be a family physician or a nurse or a social worker, but there needs to be someone.

We have to resolve our problem of waiting times for appointments and assessments (for autism, for example), for operations, and for being seen in hospital emergency clinics. We need to achieve what we have promised: that patients with less than major problems be diverted from hospital emergency clinics to groups of family physicians and to nurse practitioners. We need to find the human and material resources and the management efficiency to make expensive facilities – operating rooms, test centres, sophisticated imaging machinery – functional through nights and weekends. We need to make the whole system more humanly responsive.

Our health care system is based on universality, and it therefore theoretically covers virtually all necessary care. The fact is, however, that there is a significant private sector – this is essentially true of all developed countries – and we need to find the right balance and the right coordination with it. We need to change the focus of the debate: from principles and generalities to "What are *we* – notably physicians – going to do better, so that our patients will get more timely care?" The *quality* of that care, once the patient receives it, is extremely good.

## The Environment

There is more environmental awareness than ever before, yet there are still people who challenge the scientific evidence that we humans are contributing dangerously to climate change and must take major steps to halt and, hopefully, reverse the process. We are doing a fair amount of recycling, but we need to do even more. We are only scratching the surface of composting as a means of returning organic materials to nature. Industries are more sensitive and more responsible than in the past, but their cooperation still needs to be prodded by legislation and government action.

Longevity has increased impressively, despite the chemical substances we introduce by the hundreds every year into the environment which provides our air, our food, and our water. We cannot allow these substances to be disseminated untested, and we are not yet testing them adequately for their possible effects on children and on pregnant mothers and their growing fetuses. Nor are we paying sufficient attention to the possibility that children's growing tissues may react differently to pollutants from the way the mature organs of adults do. All of these concerns need to be in the forefront of our minds. Our dependence on fossil fuels endangers our planet in the long term. Alternative sources of energy, and sustainable development in every field, need our urgent and intelligent attention.

## Interreligious Relations

In interreligious relations we have come a very long way since World War II. We have changed to a considerable degree the whole nature of such relations. The greatest progress has been in the reciprocal understanding and mutual respect between Christians and Jews. We are looking at our shared history, and interpreting and understanding it, differently and more positively from the way we did for two millennia. I believe – and I hope that I am right – that this change is irreversible.

What we have not yet done sufficiently is to cause what we have worked out in high places to filter down to grassroots clergy and grassroots parishioners. I have assumed this effort in a small way as a personal challenge, and I hope that each person involved in dialogue will do the same.

Antisemitism, however, although greatly diminished and indeed marginalized in countries like Canada, is still a troubling phenomenon in other parts of the world. The State of Israel has become a lightning rod for criticism, and although some people carefully separate that criticism from genuine commitment to interreligious relations, not everyone does. The Jewish community cannot help but react. That community, solidly Canadian, cares a great deal about Israel. Israel is not perfect – it is one of the most self-critical societies in the entire world – but I must be frank: some anti-Israel rhetoric is an expression of antisemitism. It is primarily against this that the Jewish community reacts.

Multi-faith conversation is more widespread than ever before. There are few bilateral relationships that have the specificity and historical context of Christian-Jewish dialogue, and multi-faith subject matter tends to be broad and fundamental: peace, poverty, environmental protection. To the extent that this broad focus leads to joint social action, it is a valuable one. Dialogue with the Muslim world is a pressing necessity, infused with the hope that those who are open to it, not extremists, will be the determining influence in the future of the world.

A growing challenge is the secularization of Western society. Dialogue between the secular and the religiously committed has barely begun, but it seems clear that the two worlds share basic human values and that mutual respect and understanding between them is every bit as important as between any two religions.

From a personal point of view, I – and much less my parents and my grandparents – never thought, back in the 1930s, that a day would come when the principal of McGill, Bernard Shapiro, would sit down with the publisher of *The Gazette*,

Michael Goldbloom. A religiously committed person would say, "God be praised."

*English and French*

The English-speaking community of Quebec has come a very long way. This profoundly significant evolution is widely unrecognized in the French-speaking community. Indeed, there are conspicuous people who do not *want* to recognize it, who want *not* to recognize it. It is time that the English-speaking community stops being perceived as the antagonist; that it comes to be embraced as a partner in the building of tomorrow's Quebec, a partner effectively able and willing – indeed, eager – to do so in French, while remaining an integral community.

It is time that the institutions of the English-speaking community – universities and schools, hospitals and other agencies – be accorded an assured future; that they be recognized as two-language institutions with a noble record of contributing to Quebec society. It is time that anglophones of all origins be admissible to English-language schools; their small additional numbers will be significant for those schools and a negligible deprivation for the much larger French-speaking system. It is time that the French-speaking majority, concerned about their demographics, recognize that English-speaking Quebecers are equally concerned about theirs. It is time for fairness. I pray for linguistic harmony – which is appreciably greater than it was forty and less years ago – and for a future of shared commitment to the common good. I pray for reciprocal insight.

*Quebec and Canada*

Of all the bridge-building challenges, that between Quebec and Canada is the most difficult. The desire of many Quebecers for sovereignty is driven by the conviction that this province has been hampered, even hamstrung, in its efforts to be itself. It is my fraternal and caring feeling that the relationship has had many more positives than negatives, that this will continue, and that Quebec has achieved within Canada a considerable degree of decision-making ability and of presence on the world stage – indeed, more autonomy than any other province.

I hear and understand my sovereignist colleagues. I have always felt, as Richard Guay said, a genuine mutual respect across the aisle. I am committed to moving forward together. I am also concerned about the indifference, and sometimes hostility, of the rest of Canada. Very fundamentally, I am troubled by our two differing – indeed, opposing – visions of Canada, by our different interpretations of our history. For most English-speaking Canadians, especially outside Quebec, Canada is a union of ten equal provinces. For French-speaking Canadians, not only Quebecers, Confederation was an agreement between two peoples, one English-speaking and one French-speaking, and that duality is the nature of our country. The reciprocal reconciliation of this divergence has been a significant purpose of my life.

I look back over these ninety-plus years, and I have minimal nostalgia for the "good old days." Those "old days" would never have allowed me to be what I have been, to contribute what I have been privileged to contribute. I am deeply, deeply grateful, and I regard the future with hope.

My watchword has been *une politique de présence* – being present wherever and whenever possible. My message to the next generations is simple: Be present. Be engaged. Be constructive.

Tennyson concludes "Ulysses" with these words:

> Tho' much is taken, much abides; and tho'
> We are not now that strength which in old days
> Moved earth and heaven, that which we are, we are:
> One equal temper of heroic hearts,
> Made weak by time and fate, but strong in will
> To strive, to seek, to find, and not to yield.

It has been quite an odyssey.

# Afterword

JONATHAN GOLDBLOOM

It has not always been easy being Victor Goldbloom's son.

I was vaguely aware that my father entered provincial politics because of his commitment to medicare. He had come to the conclusion that the only way he could help to advance the recommendations that he had developed through his work with the College of Physicians and Surgeons was by being part of the political process. Yet when the Liberals were elected in 1970, Claude Castonguay, not my father, was named Minister of Health, and he had little to do with the drafting of legislation. Nonetheless, physicians – some of whom were long-standing family friends – were furious about the government's approach to the health system. Our family was ostracized by many of them for quite some time.

Bill 22, which limited access to English schools and in the end was much less draconian than Bill 101, also led to heated arguments wherever I went. Parents of childhood friends would not hesitate to lambast me. But I was better off than my mother, who was spat upon in the Cavendish Mall during the 1976 election campaign.

The choice I made at the time was to get involved, to criss-cross the province with my father during election campaigns and to a lesser extent while he was a minister. As I became more and more immersed in politics and public policy, my father seamlessly shifted his role from that of a teacher to a peer.

I learned a lot from him. Firstly, the importance of the politics of presence. At Liberal conventions he would help draft resolutions, offer translation services, and be at the mic during plenary sessions. As a minister he would always be on the road, meeting with municipal officials and other interested parties and endlessly dictating letters between stops. But it was more than being present. It was about listening and building bridges. As a pediatrician he would spend countless hours on the phone with anxious parents. Even when I was a young child, I noticed that he often repeated himself. He explained that you can tell when it clicks with a mother and she has fully understood the diagnosis and prescription. This is a talent that he brought to public life. It is an extraordinary ability to understand the perspectives of others and find ways to address them without compromising your own values and beliefs.

In many ways my father was a pioneer – the first Jewish cabinet minister in Quebec, the first Minister of the Environment, and the first Commissioner of Official Languages from the English-speaking minority of Quebec. One of my favourite stories is of getting on to a bus with my father at a Liberal caucus retreat in La Tuque when Louis-Philippe Lacroix, a colourful M N A from Îles de la Madeleine, shouted, "Notre W A S H est arrivé." My father explained to me that this referred to White Anglo-Saxon Hebrew.

At times, I and others would have wanted dad to be more strident and aggressive. But that was not his style. When treated badly, often by members of his own party, he would never let his anger get the better of him. When Mayor Drapeau would keep him waiting, he would simply read a book. When Lise Bacon leaked a memorandum he had written and portrayed his position in a negative light, he refrained from entering into what would have been a justifiable public squabble. In the end, this approach allowed my father to maintain cordial relations across the National Assembly floor and in many cases work on subsequent initiatives with his adversaries from both sides of the House years later.

I may have questioned his style, but I would never question his values.

Family has always been front and centre for him. Friday nights were Shabbat dinners at my grandparents' and Sunday was family lunch at home or at Moishes followed by an activity with my brother and me. When he was in Quebec City, he was our alarm clock, phoning at 7 a.m., and again at dinner time and bedtime.

Heated debates over current affairs were generally on the menu at family dinners, but we also were exposed to my father's love of sports, theatre, and music. To this day, he still does an outstanding rendition of "Lydia, Oh Lydia the Tattooed Lady" or "Casey at the Bat." And our family holiday for close to sixty years has been a trip to the Stratford Festival.

Laughter also echoed through the Goldbloom household. Dad would often hold our attention by telling one of his classic stories – many of which were slightly off-colour. But he also taught us to laugh at ourselves, taking delight in being nicknamed Papa Doc and in later years His Immensity.

A love of reading was passed on from my grandfather Alton to my father and to my siblings and me. My father travels with a small suitcase for clothes and a larger one for books. The years after he was a minister were taken up by him reading back issues of his favourite magazines from *The New Yorker* to *Atlantic Monthly* and *Sports Illustrated*. In fact, I think the highlight of my father's political career was having his photo in *Sports Illustrated* in the lead-up to the Olympics.

Whatever the role, Papa Doc quietly and without fanfare simply got the job done. This book is his book. You have to read between the lines to get a sense of people he likes and dislikes. On the other hand, you will gain a greater sense of the man, his values, and the issues that matter to him as well as the times he lived in.

# Acknowledgments

Sheila, who has lived through sixty-six plus years of what is recounted here, had to relive it all as the book was in gestation. She did so with grace and made constructive contributions.

My three children, Susan, Michael, and Jonathan, whose persuasion overcame my initial resistance and got me started writing, contributed valuable recollections and revisions. Michael became in fact my editor, repeatedly rereading the text for style and content, identifying omissions, and urging that I analyze and interpret various events and experiences rather than simply describe them.

Michael's super-competent executive assistant, Denise Lauzière, was the trusted custodian of the text in both languages, patiently integrating the changes and additions that arose from the polishing process.

Elizabeth Hulse, McGill-Queen's copyeditor and fact-checker extraordinaire, diplomatically coped with my pride of authorship as she brought her professional skills to bear on the book.

Jean Duhaime, retired dean of Religious Studies at the Université de Montréal, and his wife, Paule-Renée Villeneuve, who is a professional linguist, proved their long and valued friendship by kindly reading the French text.

Most of the photographs are from the Goldbloom family collections. For those which are not, we have sought to identify the photographer and give professional credit. In any instance where we have not succeeded, we would be pleased to provide the correction in any subsequent printing.